D1332695

A

John McEwen

WHO OWNS SCOTLAND?

A Study in Land Ownership

For Margaret

EDINBURGH
EUSPB

ACKNOWLEDGEMENTS

I am indebted to many for help and encouragement but must mention the following:

David and Michele Moody for typing, map, graph, many suggestions and the index.

John McGrath for his encouraging and sólid foreword.

Gordon Brown for starting me off in the Red Paper on Scotland and pressing me to go further.

My publishers, EUSPB, and friend, Bill Campbell, for guidance.

My granddaughter, Jenny, for checking the tables.

Typeset 10/12 Times by EUSPB

Printed in Scotland by Lindsay & Co. Ltd., Edinburgh

Foreword

We live in the age of the multi-national corporation. In twenty years time, we are told, 200 major corporations will dominate the economy of the entire capitalist world. National Governments, national frontiers are becoming increasingly meaningless as these giants leap over them in pursuit of profit and expansion.

The constitution of the ruling classes is changing from one of the domination of owners and industrialists, to the domination of non-owning managers operating in many countries, controlling many industries. Why, when this is going on, should we pay attention to the throw-back to feudal times that lingers on in the land-ownership patterns of Scotland?

For many small- and middle-class farmers, the actual ownership of the land is becoming increasingly meaningless. As they find themselves at the mercy of the monopolies that control their input needs, and control the prices of their output, they find themselves working more and more as servants of the market, managing the land on behalf of stronger economic forces outside their control. The biggest profit from land in many parts is not for those who reap and sow, but for property speculators, who buy and sell land, often without even walking on it — sometimes without even entering the country. Why, in the circumstances, bother about the "wildnerness" of Scotland, and how many acres of it the latest generation of an ancient family has managed to cling to?

There seem to me to be two main reasons — doubtless there are many more. The first is that examining the land-ownership structure tells us a lot about Scotland. It points to a history which is significantly different from that of neighbouring nations, and it establishes that the consequences of that history are with us today, and should affect our thinking about Scotland and its particular problems.

Scotland, to put it crudely, did not have its own bourgeois

revolution — it inherited the fruits of the English one by the Act of Union. But this Act and the subsequent growth of Scottish capital was carefully 'managed' by the Scottish aristocracy. The aristocrats had accumulated their own wealth not because they were skilful merchants, but because they owned vast acres of land. Through ownership of mineral rights and/or careful investment of their capital, and/or very convenient marriages, plus wily use of their strong political position, they remained in the forefront of the new capitalist class. This allowed them to retain their vast estates, and the quasi-feudal relationships that went with them, even to this day.

This extraordinary blend of go-getting capitalist in London and archaic 'seigneur' at home still characterises many of the landowners of Scotland; those whose capital has failed them on the Stock Exchange seem to retain even more archaic attitudes on their estates — perhaps to compensate for their lack of real power in the modern world. The result, either way, is that a massive proportion of Scottish land resources remains in the hands of a small group of people. Most of them lack either the desire, or the capital, to bring it into the 20th century. To understand the size of the problem we need to know what John McEwen has struggled to establish in this book. Then we need to know the full facts about land use — the potential, and the actual productivity.

It is shameful that no Government agency has provided *any* of this information, save a census over a century ago. It is a sign that no Government so far has bothered to investigate the *specific* problems of Scotland, which have arisen from its history, and developed in a different way from the problems of the rest of the U.K. However, even in the absence of the rest of the research, many would give a shrewd guess that the land in Scotland is in much the same situation as the coal-miners before they were nationalised — archaically run, unprofitable, under-capitalised and socially disastrous. Even by these pragmatic standards, there seems to be a clear case for government intervention.

But there is a second reason why this research into land-ownership in Scotland is important. That is: people live on, and by, this land. The economic life of three-quarters of Scotland is determined by the use to which the land is put. Apart from the national trauma of the Clearances, there has been, ever since, an erosion of population, and a destruction of communities, not only in the Highlands but in many other areas as well, due to mis-use of the land. The lives of

2

millions of people have been affected by decisions taken by landowners, decisions over which the people have no control — even through their elected representatives, local or national. If ever anything betrays the hypocritical sham of bourgeois democracy, this situation does.

The use to which land is put is of vital concern to *all* those who live on it, or by its potential. The decision to divert capital from its development into higher-yielding investments elsewhere cannot be taken by one person. Still less can the decision to keep it going as a grouse-moor or deer-forest. The decision to sell it to some other private individual with cash but no stated policy amounts to a denial of basic rights to whole communities, indeed to the whole of society.

So nationalisation after the "coal-miners" model is clearly not enough (nor was it for the miners). The land needs to be nationalised in order to put it under local community control, with capital assistance, guidance information and technical help from a central authority. This land authority should co-ordinate the massive amount of research currently going on into land use, and have an overall strategy for developing all the land to its full potential. Ironically, the historical processes that allowed the land to be preserved in large estates, make the transfer of ownership and control much easier.

John McEwen, in this book, has begun the process of revealing the facts — not simply of our scandalous inheritance from the past, but also the facts that will indicate a course to a better future. It has been a laborious, frustrating and exhausting job, but well worth all his effort, and we should all be extremely grateful to him. As Mary McPherson said in the 1880's, "there is gold in the land beneath your feet": now in the 1970's is the time to take down the Keep Out signs, and start digging. Then perhaps "Every person will have a place".

John McGrath

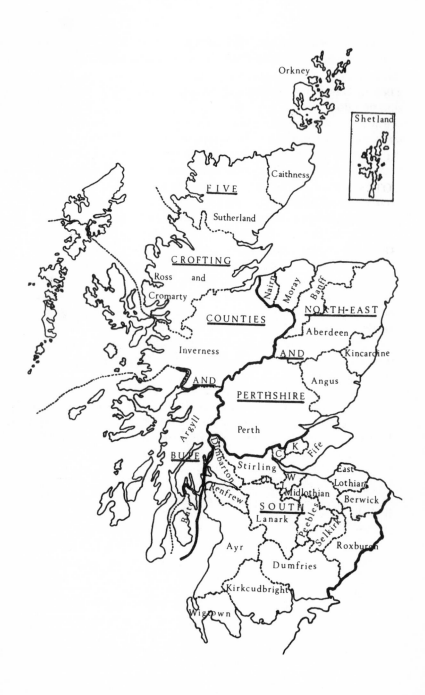

Contents

	page
FOREWORD by John McGrath	1
INTRODUCTION by John McEwen	7
EXPLANATIONS	8
AUTIOBIOGRAPHY by John McEwen	9
BACKGROUND AND SOURCES	13
GENERAL TABLE: LANDOWNERSHIP IN SCOTLAND	17
SCOTLAND'S 100 LARGEST LANDOWNERS	18
CROFTING COUNTIES REGION WEST	21
SUMMARY FOR FIVE CROFTING COUNTIES PLUS BUTE	39
THE NORTH-EASTERN COUNTIES	41
SUMMARY FOR THE NORTH-EAST PLUS PERTHSHIRE	57
THE SOUTHERN COUNTIES	59
SUMMARY FOR THE SOUTH	85
NUMBER OF ESTATES AND ACREAGES PER REGION	86
SUMMARY OF PRIVATE ESTATES IN THREE REGIONS	87
FINAL SUMMARIES	88
MANAGEMENT AND HUSBANDRY OF OUR LAND	
(i) Private Enterprise in Forestry	90
(ii) The Forestry Commission	93
(iii) Forestry Education & Careers	97
(iv) The Commission's Failures	99
(v) Private Enterprise in Agriculture	104
(vi) Aids for Agriculture	106
(vii) Little Neddies and The Swann Report	108
(viii) Game	110
(ix) Highlands & Islands Development Board	113
PRESCRIPTION	115
APPENDICES	119

Introduction

I have just completed (1st April 1977), from Millman's maps (see note on these later), the acreages of privately owned estates from the largest one of 270,000 acres, owned by the Duke of Buccleuch, down to those of 1,000 acres, and in all totalling 1,739 estates, And now I ask myself on the 1st of April if it has been a 'gowk's errand'.

In the last twenty-five to thirty years my deep concern with land, land use and land ownership has been looked on by many of my socialist friends with amazement and forebearance, and today men like Bruce Millan still maintain that a land register of all our landlords and their estate acreages down to say 500 acres is of no value. It may have been a gowk's errand, but I have gone on with it and the quite big task is completed; and it is now left for the judgment of others to decide whether it has been worthwhile or not.

Personally, I think my investigations (made possible by Dr Millman's maps) have been very much worthwhile, but the point must be stressed that the acreages produced are not as exact as they should and would be with mapping by the Ordnance Survey Department. The need for an official register, despite what Secretaries of State for Scotland say, is obvious and as soon as completed it must be kept up-to-date until the full nationalisation of all land will cancel out the need for such a register.

And now I have to get down to work and show the terrific mess into which landlords in Scotland have landed us. Firstly, their inadequate husbandry in agriculture sticks out a mile, particularly in the huge area of their 10,000,000 acres of rough grazings—it always has been so and still is. Secondly, in forestry with their 200/300 years practice I have not seen a single private estate with well managed woodlands: so very different from the excellent silviculture found all over Scotland in our state forests with only 50 odd years experience behind them. Thirdly, the sadistic obsession with game resulting in the almost complete degradation of millions of acres of our land.

This state of affairs just cannot continue.

EXPLANATIONS

It should be noted that in the 1874 Register the "estimated acreage" was followed by its "Gross Annual Value". In my recordings this G.A.V. is placed, in brackets usually, immediately following the estate acreage. In the G.A.V. of such assets as coal this is clearly stated as such.

All the acreages from Millman's maps are based on his datum-line of 1970.

F.C.—Forestry Commission.

DAFS— Department of Agriculture & Fisheries for Scotland.

MAFF—Ministry of Agriculture, Fisheries & Food.

HFRO—Hill Farming Research Organisation.

HIDB—Highlands & Islands Development Board.

Tree volumes given in this book are those of the antiquated, and up to quite recently in steady constant use in the U.K. (nowhere else), "Quarter Girth" or "Hoppus" measurement. This meant that only 79 per cent of true measure, or true volume was recorded. A wily timber merchant's trick? I have often wondered. All timber was bought and sold for generations on this basis and I am quite sure many a poor landowner was quite unaware of this. Now all measurement of timber is by cubic metre.

Autobiography

My long-suffering publishers have asked me to write a short autobiography, and I feel I must comply. But, first, let me give a rather fuller picture of rural life in Scotland as I saw it ninety years ago.

My father was employed as shepherd/forester at Garth Castle, Fortingall, owned by the millionaire ship-owner, Sir Donald Currie. The house I was born in, newly built by Sir Donald, was attached to a small public hall and consisted of only two very small rooms, a downstairs kitchen and a low ceilinged attic with a skylight. The siting was peculiar, at the side of the public road, close up to the Keltneyburn bridge. The house surround was so restricted that not even a square foot was available for a garden patch. Our neighbour's house was close up against us.

Every drop of water had to be carried up the very steep slope to the house (I once rolled down this slope adjoining the path, and was only saved from drowning by bumping into a small tree on the edge of the burn). In flood, from Rannoch-side, the burn came raging and tearing through the narrow dark gorge below the house. The annual killing of our neighbour's stuck pig and its squealing till it bled to death added to the nightmarish memories I still have.

But there were compensations. I remember, one bright Spring Sunday morning — I was, perhaps, six — walking alongside the Lyon to Garth Castle Park with my father, to see his lambs. The sight of masses of crocuses, on both sides of the avenue, stretching as far as I could see, had a stunning effect on me. The joyful feeling of brightness, beauty and space remains with me still. Soon afterwards, when I was seven, our family (now with three children) moved to Castle Lachlan, Lochfyneside, belonging to the Chieftain, John Maclachlan of Maclachlan. My father was now estate over-seer.

Housing here was different — a dilapidated, rat-ridden but-and-ben with a run-down garden. Our first job — and my brother and I

9

helped in this — was to try to get rid of the hordes of rats, but finally a professional rat-catcher had to be called in from Glasgow as the Castle environs were swarming. It took him two weeks to clear them out.

After that it took several years to make the house habitable and to get the garden into a condition to produce vegetables, fruit and flowers, which my father loved. Here we had a very happy, quiet family life and it was with very mixed feelings that I went to Glasgow — on a bursary — at the age of eleven to be introduced to Secondary Education — including the blistering tawse.

I left school at fourteen, having made no great headway, and many a time I wondered what I gained in these three years away from the warmth, love and companionship of home life.

There was no outlet in the Strath for young people. For a time I did odd jobs, and then, in 1905, sped North to start my training in forestry on one of Seafield's famous estates, at Cullen. Real forestry training was absent, but not so perpetual motion: working from seven to six every day of the week (except Sunday and with slightly shorter hours in mid-winter) every day of the year except for two "fast" days and New Year's day — being kept on tenterhooks on Hogmanay as to whether we would get an extra couple of hours off. After two years I went to Altyre Estate, Forres, where things were more civilised — we had the Saturday half-day.

In 1908 I took up a course in the Royal Botanic Garden, Edinburgh — working from six till five in the summer and a bit less in winter. This course gave evening classes in land surveying, botany, geology, chemistry etc. and I also took classes in forestry, maths., and English in the Agricultural and Heriot Watt Colleges. Two years there were followed by two in the Glasgow Parks, when again I took evening classes.

By this time I was ready for a charge job, but the only thing open to me was back in private estates, and though I was offered quite attractive posts, nothing would induce me to go. I took a wild step — into contracting — felling and horse-work — in the home timber trade. This was pure slavery but I had to stick to it.

In 1914 I married Bell Thomson whom I had met in 1910 when we were both helping with the Pollokshields U.F. Church Mission in the Glasgow slums. We settled in a pleasant wee house in Bannockburn.

Then, in 1917, I gave up contracting and took a job with James Jones, Timber Merchants of Larbert, to gain some inside knowledge of saw-milling. I cycled to Larbert each day and twice a week also cycled into Stirling to attend evening classes — chemistry and physics. I was promoted to manager of one of Jones's outside mills, but this job was not satisfying to me.

The formation of the Forestry Commission in 1919 and the start of State forestry was the finest thing that ever happened in land-use in the U.K. The establishment of young plantations and forests was always my objective in life, and here it came. I was appointed forester-in-charge in the Aberdeen Division (now Conservancy) and pioneered in its first forest, Monaughty near Elgin. I remained in this district until 1928 during which time I also started off Teindland and Speymouth (Ordiequish) Forests plus the twenty acre Altonside distributing nursery, where in the spring of 1924 we lined out seven million plants, employing eighty men and women and clearing out the Elgin Labour Exchange. About 1922 I also organised the Commission's foresters-in-charge in Scotland into the Workers' Trade Union (now incorporated in the TGWU) and later represented them at the Whitley Council, appealing for improved conditions.

In 1928 I was promoted to District Officer and transferred to North Wales, but only for a few months, as, in December, I was appointed Senior Inspector to the Forestry Department Eire and moved across before the end of the year. This post I, most regretfully, had to give up after two and a quarter years for family health reasons, though pressed to remain, and came back to Scotland. I had had a big job in Eire with charge of forests from Donegal to Cork, which I did enjoy.

For the next ten years I was in the wilderness during the depression — trying to make a living in any way possible, but in 1941 I returned to timber, joining the Home Grown Timber Department of the Board of Trade as a works officer. In 1945 I was again thrown out of work. However, I got tied up with my good friend, Frank Scott, in consultancy and timber valuation work and we worked closely together until he retired. I have carried on on my own up to the present. One of my last big timber sales — a small estate near Perth — in 1974, was to my old employers, Jones of Larbert, who paid a peak price, £39,250 plus 10 per cent V.A.T. for twenty six acres of forty five year old mixed conifers. I had coddled this stand for over twenty years and had planned, and completed, at very low cost — £5,000 — an internal road system which enabled Messrs. Jones to load fifteen-ton lorries and clear off their timber at conveyor-belt

11

speed. This year I am closing my books, and taking up the painting of trees.

In 1966, my wife Bell died, and I expected to live alone for the rest of my life. But, at a Fabian weekend school at Aberfoyle, I met Margaret Miller, whose husband Andrew had been killed during the war. We were married in 1967 and have had ten years of absolute joy. Instead of being a lonely old character I have acquired not only a wife but also a daughter, a son-in-law and five lively grand-children.

Background and Sources

Millions of words have been written on Scotland's land, its owners, what have you. I have written thousands myself and the ground I am now covering is a temptation to continue doing so. However, I am not being tempted: what I am now offering is a cut-and-dried written statement along with these lists from Millman's maps which I hope may help, even in a small way, to end the tragic state into which our precious asset, land, has fallen.

All my life I have been close to the land. There is, however, nothing soft or sentimental in my attitude towards it, rather a deep growing concern over these sixty years, for the way in which it has been managed, leading to its present degraded, underdeveloped condition. This is due to the fact of ownership, in the main, by powerful, selfish, anti-social landlords. I was not alone. In 1910 Tom Johnston's 'Our Scots Noble Families' was published, and its effect on all thinking, forward-looking people was immediate and terrific. It still is, and it is a must for anyone deeply concerned about land, its ownership and use. Several copies have passed through my hands.

For myself, I can only repeat my growing concern on this vital matter; as I got older, I kept trying to find a way to show up the stranglehold of our Scottish landlords and have it completely smashed.

Then in 1967 a way was opened up when our local Perth and Kinross Fabian Society decided to discover who were the landowners of Perthshire. We thought it would be a simple project to complete. It took us four years' gruelling work and even then we did not come near completing the task. Our pamphlet, 'The Acreocracy of Perthshire — Who Owns Our Land?' (written by Alasdair Steven in conjunction with a small committee) published in 1971 tells how we were thwarted and obstructed in our researches, but does not tell the circuitous way in which some of our information was obtained. We thought we had done quite a good job of work in which we were able to trace thirty-one owners who owned from 130,000 acres down to 10,000 acres giving a total of 727,500 acres out of the 1,600,000 acres for the county. 'Acreocracy' has had in a quiet way, a world-wide circulation, and the Society remains proud of carrying out this pioneer work, but stopped there. I was not really satisfied however.

At the same time as we were working on Perthshire, Roger Millman (now Dr. Millman) of Aberdeen University was carrying on similar work, but in a very much bigger way, in the Crofting Counties and Perthshire in what he terms 'marking the "marches" (boundaries) of their private estates'.

These estate boundaries were marked on 1″ Ordnance Survey sheets with the name of the estate written clearly within this boundary. Acreages of estates were not attempted, and, I feel sure, would have been frowned on by our landlords.

A separate index card was completed for each estate stating the name of the owner. This was a terrific break-through — what I had been waiting for in fact. In 1972 I discovered that these original marked maps and cards had been lodged with the Record Office, Register House, Edinburgh, and that copies could be bought. Perthshire was my first objective. I sent for the relevant maps and cards and began to check-up on 'Acreocracy'. The first task was to define the county boundary — very difficult as the county boundaries were frequently covered completely by the heavy pencilling of estate boundaries. (This became much more time-consuming in the South when I came to deal with those maps). I marked county boundaries in red, roads yellow, railways brown, significant areas of water blue, then re-defined every estate boundary clearly in black, so that measuring could be done quickly. The actual assessment of acreage using the planimeter was by far the easiest and most pleasant part of the whole operation, but had to be done carefully and as accurately as possible. Each acreage was written within the boundary as it was measured, the estate and its acreage then being linked up with its owner(s) as shown in the index inventory cards. The fact that photostat copies were not true to the 1″ to the mile scale stated on them caused delay, when I discovered that my total for the county (Perthshire) was far too low. I was foxed but my friend Keith Openshaw came to visit us just then and, with his help, my planimeter was adjusted as near as possible to the photostat scales, not giving guaranteed accurate results but as near as did not matter.

Nowadays Register House warns customers that these maps are not to scale, but I find it even more annoying that there are differences in scales between sheets even in one estate. Surely they could do better duplication than this on such very important maps. Eventually, I did get Perthshire landowners listed — and my appetite was whetted for more.

I ordered all the Five Crofting Counties mainland maps, and later the island ones for these counties. I ploughed through all these for years — until 1975 when Gordon Brown, the outstanding student Rector of Edinburgh University asked if I would send the work to him for inclusion in 'The Red Paper on Scotland' which he was then editing for publication by EUSPB. This I was proud to do, though I was pushed for time to get the article 'Highland Landlordism' into shape.

The itch was soon on me again. I remembered the forestry work I had done in the North East — from Nairn to Angus, and sent for maps and index sheets for these counties. Procedure was the same as for the West, but more difficult and slower, though just as interesting. This, when completed, I thought, put paid to my work. But did it? One day quite soon after this, Margaret, my wife, and I looked at each other and said: 'What about completing the South?'.

The result was our home again being inundated with maps and index sheets (sheets £91) and more pain. I thought I knew the technique! But from beginning to end I was constantly in trouble trying to get the counties linked. Try Berwick. Furthermore, the surveying of this region was not of the quality of the other two regions, and much messier. When, having finished these 18 counties I wrote to Register House asking for Orkney and Shetland, they must have been fed up with my enquiries, and pretty glad to be able to tell me that Millman had not done these islands. I also was glad and sorry.

The following lists show the ownership position at 1970. Changes in ownership are always taking place, but I am not attempting to keep any of this work up-to-date: that would be the function of an official land register.

With regard to the 'notes' which I have given against each county, those with the date 1874 (datum line for that period) are taken from the Government list of statistics in their publication of that year entitled 'Lands and Heritages'. Besides acreages there is also stated the Gross Annual Value of each property, and this, in my list, is given

15

within brackets (£).
The 1970 dating is Roger Millman's datum line for that period.

OUR LAND IN SCOTLAND
How it is Owned
Total Area 19,068,807 acres

Private Owned (in round figures)

In Estates down to 1,000 acres .... 12,000,000 acres
In Estates under 1,000 acres .... 4,500,000 acres

Total: 16,500,000 acres

State Owned

Forestry Commission .... 1,895,500 acres
Dept. of Agriculture .... 445,800 acres
British Railways .... 45,000 acres
National Coal Board .... 49,000 acres
Defence .... 48,900 acres

Total: 2,500,000 acres

Landlordism in Scotland:
The Top 100 Landowners

(1970)

Owners	Estates	Acres
Duke of Buccleuch	Buccleuch Estates	277,000
Wills Family	Wills Estates	263,000
Lord Seafield	Seafield Estates	185,000
Countess of Sutherland	Sutherland Estates	158,000
Duke of Atholl	Atholl Estates	130,000
Capt. A. A. C. Farquharson	Invercauld Estates	119,000
Duke of Westminster	Westminster Estates	113,000
British Aluminium Ltd.	British Aluminium Estates	110,000
Lord Stair	Stair Estates	110,000
Sir D. Cameron	Lochiel Estates	98,000
Duke of Roxburgh	Roxburgh Estates	96,000
E. H. Vestey	Vestey Estates	93,000
S. Uist Estates Ltd.	S. Uist Estates	92,000
Lord Cowdray	Cowdray Estates	88,000
Liberton Properties Ltd.	Big House Estates	85,000
	Uig Crofters Estates,	
Benmore Estates Ltd.	Benmore Estates	79,000
Lord Lovat	Lovat Estates	76,000
Morrison family (distillers)	Islay Estates	75,000
Duke of Argyll	Argyll Estates	74,000
Stornoway Trust	Stornoway Estates	65,000
Earl of Ancaster	Drummond Castle	65,000
Michael Berry	Altnaharra Estates	63,000
Maj. Hereward Wake	Amhuinnsuidhe	63,000
Ross Estates Ltd. (Ross family)	Balnagowan	61,000
Maj. T. G. Moncrieff	Strathmore Estates	60,000
Sir H. P. MacKenzie	Gairloch Estates	58,000
Sir Alec Douglas Home	Douglas Home Estates	54,000
Sinclair family Trust	Ulbster Estates	53,000
Galston Estates Ltd.	Galston Lodge	52,000
Fothringham family	Fothringham Estates	52,000
Harlay & Jones (Investors) Ltd.	Mar Lodge	52,000
R. Fleming	Blackmount	51,000
Lord Granville	N. Uist Estates	50,000
Sir E. W. Gladstone	Fasque	48,000
Duke of Portland	Langwell	48,000
Brig. Colvin	Camusericht	45,000
Economic Forestry Ltd.	E.F.G. Estates	44,000
Lord Dalhousie	Dalhousie Estates	44,000
Lord Thorneycroft	Eiskin	44,000
Lord Wemyss	Wemyss Estates	44,000
Sir I. Colquhoun	Luss Estates	43,000
Sir O. Crosswaithe-Eyre	Knoydart	43,000
Sir W. P. Ramsden	Ardverikie	43,000
Barvas Estates Ltd.	Barvas Estates	42,000
Lord MacDonald	Sleat Estates	42,000

Owner(s)	Estates	Acres
Jura Ltd. (Astor)	Tarbert (Jura)	41,000
J. E. Elliot (Langholm)	Dunfelling Estates	40,000
Mrs J. B. W. Tyser	Gordon Bush	40,000
Lord Burton	Dochfour Estates	39,000
Lord Cawdor	Cawdor Estates	39,000
W. Gordon	Lude and Arrisdale	39,000
V. G. Balan	Forsinard	38,000
Maj. Buchanan-Jardine & others	Castlemilk Estates	36,000
I. MacPherson	Attadale	36,000
Ardtornish Estate Ltd.	Ardtornish	35,000
The Queen	Balmoral Estates	35,000
R. F. T. Foljambe	Malness	35,000
J. MacLeod of MacLeod	Dunvegan	35,000
M. S. M. Threipland	Toftingall, Waas, Dale	34,000
A. B. L.Munro-Ferguson	Novar Estates	34,000
A. S., A. F., M. M. Roger	Dundonnell	33,000
Lord Airlie	Airlie Estates	32,000
Miss E. J. M. Douglas	Kililian	32,000
J. F. Robinson	Monagail	32,000
J. M. Guthrie	Conaglen	31,000
Noble family	Ardkinglass	31,000
J. C. & P. Wilson	Garrogie & Loch Rosque	31,000
Eagle Star Ins. Co. Ltd.	Eagle Star Estates	30,000
Lochluichart Estates Ltd.	Kinlochluichart	29,000
H. & H. Blythe	Dunbeath	28,000
The late Lord Glentanar	Glentanar	27,000
Mrs E. E. Bonnington Wood	Salachy	27,000
Carloway Estates Ltd.	Carloway	27,000
Capt. Sandison	Glentromie	27,000
The Lady Mary Boscawan	Dougne	27,000
Trustees of R. Midwood	Syre	26,000
Lord Roseberry	Dalmeny Estates	25,000
Lord Bute	Bute Estates	25,000
Mr & Mrs Balfour	Balbirnie & Scourie	25,000
Maj. I. M. Scobie	Rhidderoch	25,000
Fyvie Settlement Trust alias A. G. Forbes	Fyvie	25,000
Auchentoul Estates Co.	Auchentoul	24,000
Sir Alan Wigan	Borrobol	24,000
Rattray Discretionary Trust	Haddo-Rattray	24,000
Lady McCorquodale	Gruinard	24,000
Lord Leverhulme	Badanloch	23,000
E. J. & R. N. Lowes	Glenfalloch	23,000
R. Williams	Strathvaich	23,000
A. Carlton Greg	Lochcarron	23,000
Mrs Barker & Mrs Kershaw	Soval	23,000
Stewarts Estates Aberdeen Ltd.	Slains Castle	23,000
Lord Linlithgow	Linlithgow Estates	23,000
Mrs M. Garton	Loch Merkland	23,000
Parc Crofters Estates Ltd.	Parc Crofters Estate	23,000
Capt. A. A. Ramsay	Mar	23,000
M. J. Beecher	Arisaig	23,000
Mrs A. R. Nelson	Ardlussa	22,000

19

Owner(s)	Estates	Acres
Taylor Bros.	Abernethy (Inverness)	22,000
T. L. Girvan	W. Ceannacroe	22,000
Lord Ailsa	Cassilis Estates	21,000

CROFTING COUNTIES REGION WEST

This region has 6 counties from Caithness to Argyll and Bute.

There are 536 private estates down to 1,000 acres with 6,153,400 acres.

> Caithness
> Sutherland
> Ross and Cromarty
> Inverness
> Argyll
> Bute

Five Crofting Counties plus Bute

CAITHNESS

In 1874, landowners with the family name of Sinclair held 187,000 out of the county's 471,000 acres, bringing in £33,000 gross annual value. This family remains as the largest owner in 1970 with 52,600 acres.

The Duke of Portland still owns 48,000 acres, as against 81,000 (£8,000) in 1874. On the other hand, the Anstruthers' (from Fife) estate drops from 37,000 (£6,000) to 15,300 acres.

Caithness remains a county of large estates, with 17 landlords owning 304, 100 acres.

CAITHNESS

Land area	438,943
Inland water	7,177

Estates down to 5,000 acres

Owner	Estate	Acres
Sinclair Family Trust	Ulbster	52,600
Duke of Portland	Langwell, Braemore Ests.	48,000
N. S. M. Threipland	Waas, Dale, Toftingall	33,800
H. and H. Blythe	Dunbeath	27,500
Tr. of D. C. Duff Sutherland Dunbar	Hempriggs	17,700
Unknown	Glutt	16,900
Sir R. H. Anstruther	Watten	15,300
Sir R. & Lady I. Holmes Black	Shurrery	14,500
J. S. Spencer Thomas	Freswick	13,000
Lt. Col. H. B. Taylor	Sandside	12,600
Clare College, Cambridge	Mey	10,800
Unknown	Dorrery	9,500
Thrumster Ests. Ltd.	Thrumster	8,100
John Sinclair	Clyth Mains	7,700
Mrs A. P. Pottinger	Greenland	5,500
Mr & Mrs J. W. Sutherland	Granton Mains	5,500
E. & J. Darmaday	Camster	5,100

Totals of Estates down to 5,000 acres
17 Estates — 304,100 acres

Estates 5,000 to 1,000 acres

Between	5,000 and 4,000 acres:	4:	18,000 acres
	4,000 and 3,000 acres:	4:	12,000 acres
	3,000 and 2,000 acres:	3:	6,600 acres
	2,000 and 1,000 acres:	6:	9,500 acres

Totals of Estates 5,000 to 1,000 acres
17 Estates — 46,100 acres

Summary

Estates between	75,000 and 50,000 acres:	1:	52,600 acres
	50,000 and 40,000 acres:	1:	48,000 acres
	40,000 and 30,000 acres:	1:	33,800 acres
	30,000 and 20,000 acres:	1:	27,500 acres
	20,000 and 10,000 acres:	7:	100,800 acres
	10,000 and 5,000 acres:	6:	41,400 acres
	5,000 and 1,000 acres:	17:	46,100 acres

Grand Total of Estates down to 1,000 acres
34 Estates — 350,200 acres

Total land area of county .... 438,943 acres

Total area of private Estates down to 1,000 acres .... 350,200 acres

SUTHERLAND

In 1874 this was the county of extremes. The Duke of Sutherland with 1,180,000 acres worth £56,400 annually had a relative at Skibo Castle with 21,000 acres worth £32,000. In 1970 the present Duke owns no land here, but the estate remains in the family. The Countess of Sutherland holds 123,500 acres and, as Mrs Janson, a further 34,500 acres — a big fall, but still comfortable.

In 1874 there was not room in Sutherland for any other really big landlords; however, the Mathesons of Ross-shire, the adjoining county, had managed to grasp 18,500 acres, but in both counties the Mathesons have disappeared by 1970. The vacuum thus created in the breaking-up of these huge estates allowed outsiders to come in, led by the Duke of Westminster with his present holding of 112,700 acres. This estate was much bigger up to about 1967, when

23

considerable areas were again sold off, such as Scourie (16,200 acres) now in the hands of Mr and Mrs Balfour who also own a big chunk of the most valuable land in Fife. It would seem that these new owners are even more difficult to live with than the previous ones, which would seem impossible.

Their M.P., Mr R. MacLennan complains in the House of Commons (Hansard 3rd July '73) that ". . . the Chairman of the Scottish Countryside Commission, Mrs Balfour, who is a constituent of mine, has spoken of a large area in Sutherland which she owns — the estate of Scourie — as being nothing but rock and water, and therefore, incapable either of being developed or of providing any sort of employment. On the face of it, that is an extraordinary insensitive description of one of the most interesting ecological areas in the country and a neglect of the possible interests of the community in the nature conservation of that area.

I quote that example because it is known to me, and reflects an attitude of mind which one would not expect to see in a person fulfilling such an important public office in Scotland — a 'keep out' attitude, because the area is of relatively little interest. Perhaps it is because she has a personal interest in the area that she does not appreciate the public interest in it".

Besides the above, there are new landlords such as Vestey with 81,400 acres (and 11,700 in Ross) along with 15 others owning from 20,000 to 60,000 acres each. In 1970 I saw a good deal of Vestey's land; it is not all poor. The valuable Stoer section, for instance, was scandalously underdeveloped. My friend David MacLennan (of 7:84 Theatre Group) knows the county intimately and he, too, is sad at the thought of its valuable glens going further and further to wreck. Most of the land is held for sport, and so the less developed and the less populated it is the better. It suits absentee landlordism admirably.

On the east side of the county there is good husbandry, but this covers a comparatively small part of the county, so that the great bulk of its 1¼ million acres is just degraded.

SUTHERLAND

Land area:	Mainland	1,295,062 acres	1,297,803 acres
	Islands	2,741 acres	
Inland water:	Mainland	47,721 acres	47,727 acres
	Islands	6 acres	

Estates down to 5,000 acres

Owner	Estate	Acres
Countess of Sutherland	Sutherland Ests.	123,500
Duke of Westminster	Reay, Kylestrome	112,700
E. H. Vestey	Lochinver, Assynt	81,400
Michael Berry	Altnaharra, Clerbig	62,300
Maj. T. G. Moncrieff	Strathmore Ests.	60,000
Benmore Ests. Ltd.	Benmore	44,100
J. E. Elliot (Langholm)	Dunfelling Ests.	40,000
Mrs J. B. W. Tyser	Gordonbush	40,000
Liberton Properties	Bighouse	38,300
V. G. Balan	Forsinard	37,800
R. F. T. Foljambe	Hope, Malness	34,500
Mrs E. M. Janson	Delnessie Ests.	34,500
Mrs E. E. Bonnington Wood	Sallachy	26,700
Tr. of R. Midwood	Syre	25,400
Auchentoul Ests. Co.	Auchentoul	24,100
Sir Adam Wigan	Borrobol	23,700
Mrs M. Garton	Loch Merkland	23,200
Vt. Leverhulme	Badanloch	22,800
Kinlochbervie Hotel	Kinlochbervie	19,700
Mr & Mrs Price Jenkins	Killouman	19,700
Lord Roborough	Shelpick	19,500
Lady Balfour of Inchyre	Tressary	17,600
Lady Paynter	Kildonan	17,500
Mr & Mrs Balfour	Scourie	16,200
Gen. Osborne	Rhiemich	14,400
Torrish Co. Ltd.	Torrish	14,300
M. A. H. Fletcher	Shinness	14,100
R. M. Abel Smith	Cambusmore	13,000
Mrs E. Lloyd	Glen Cassley	9,500
P. Robinson	Smoo Lodge	9,000
Miss Upwhat	Inchnadamph	8,600
Mrs Fergusson	Gualin	8,200
Lord Rootes	Rispond	7,500
Miss N. Bradford	Tumore	7,500
Tr. Lt. Col. Negus	Invernaver	7,200
W. Palmer Sankey	Loch Assynt Lodge	5,500
G. T. Roberts	Morvich	5,100
Miss M. G. Dudgeon	Crakaig	5,000

Totals of Estates down to 5,000 acres

38 Estates —1,094,100 acres

Estates 5,000 to 1,000 acres

Between			
	5,000 and 4,000 acres:	5:	21,700 acres
	4,000 and 3,000 acres:	2	7,000 acres
	3,000 and 2,000 acres:	6:	14,000 acres
	2,000 and 1,000 acres:	2:	2,700 acres

Totals of Estates 5,000 to 1,000 acres

15 Estates— 45,400 acres

Summary

Estates of	100,000 acres and over:	2:	236,200 acres
Estates between	100,000 and 75,000 acres:	2:	81,400 acres
	75,000 and 50,000 acres:	2:	122,300 acres
	50,000 and 40,000 acres:	3:	124,100 acres
	40,000 and 30,000 acres:	4:	145,100 acres
	30,000 and 20,000 acres:	6:	145,900 acres
	20,000 and 10,000 acres:	10:	166,000 acres
	10,000 and 5,000 acres:	10:	73,100 acres
	5,000 and 1,000 acres:	15:	45,400 acres

Grand total of Estates down to 1,000 acres

53 Estates — 1,139,500 acres

Total land area of County .... 1,297, 803 acres

Total area of private Estates down to 1,000 acres .... 1,139,500 acres

ROSS AND CROMARTY

This county of around two million acres (including the islands) could quite easily have a full fledged book for itself instead of the mere insert for now.

In 1874 it certainly had no giant owner like the Sutherlands with their 1¼ million acres in the county of that name, but it did not come very far behind with the Mathesons' holding in the extreme west (Lewis) and the very valuable land in the east at Ardross, 627,00 acres (£40,000). They had bought themselves in with money made in tea. So far as Dr Millman's records go, nothing remains of this family. The MacKenzies, old-time county landlords, did not come far behind, with around 400,000 acres (£42,000). They are still in possession, but with a reduced holding of 58,000 acres. The MacKenzie chief was one of the commissioners on the 1885 Napier crofting survey. He, along with a near neighbour, Cameron of Lochiel, also a commissioner, had a powerful influence in determining that the absolute minimum was granted to the crofters. (Napier, the chairman, was also a big landowner in the South owning 7,000 acres of the most valuable land in Selkirk).

Ross of Balnagown in 1874 owned 100,000 acres (£12,652). These Rosses must have been wide — no infertile areas for them, but land of quality in the east, which gave them the above huge sum each year. A few years ago about 40,000 acres of this estate were sold. This sold off area is not identifiable. They are again in the market, April 1977. It is around here that the secretive Arabs are now settling in.

26

The Sutherlands were not content to remain in their own county, but had acquired 11,000 acres here (£12,000). Nothing of this holding is recorded in 1970.

In Applecross, Lord Middleton owned 63,000 acres (£2,000). This is now owned by the Willses (of tobacco 'fame' and friends of royalty) and has swelled to 100,000 acres. More will appear later about this family, including Lord Dulverton. Their interest is, in the main, sport, though Lord Dulverton has, for some years, appeared to be interested in forestry. He has, at Fassifern, completed a scheme of integrating agriculture and forestry — but I should like very much to know, in view of red deer invasion what his forestry costs are per acre. Red deer fencing is now deadly — not less than £3,000 a mile.

The old Highland family of Baillie (Burtons, of Bass fame) owned, last century, 32,000 acres (£9,000). Lord Burton still owns 20,000 acres in Ross. They also appeared in Inverness in 1874 and still do.

One notable, A. J. Balfour, owned 72,000 acres here in addition to his holdings at Whittinghame. No Balfour appears in the present day Ross-shire records.

The joint names of Munro and Ferguson covered the Novar estate of 40,000 acres (£3,600) and were also owners of over 7,000 acres at Raith in Fife — top quality land as shown by its Gross Annual Value of £12,300. The present owner is A. B. L. Munro Ferguson, with an Aberdeen forestry degree, who recently was reputed to have sold 'a small proportion of land' for £786,000, at Novar.

The Highland laird still demands his pound of flesh. He still owns 28,700 acres at Novar.

And finally (though there is plenty of material left) there are the two top men in the 1970 list, Whitbread with 73,100 acres and MacDonald-Buchanan 71,100 acres, well known purveyors of booze.

Whitbread is now (April 1977) in the market "offering 34 sq. miles and buyers from the Continent and the Middle East are showing most interest in paying the asking-price of £500,000" - *The Scotsman.*

ROSS & CROMARTY

Land area	Mainland	1,572,835	1,977,254 acres
	Islands	404,419	
Inland water	Mainland	48,101	72,784 acres
	Islands	24,683	

27

C

Estates down to 5,000 acres

Owner	Estate	Acres
Col. W. H. Whitbread	Letterewe	73,100
A. J. MacDonald-Buchanan	Strathconon etc.	71,100
Stornoway Trust	Stornoway Est. (Lewis)	64,300
Ross Estates Ltd.	Balnagowan	61,100
Sir H. P. Mackenzie	Gairloch	57,600
Galston Ests. Ltd.	Galston Lodge Lewis	52,200
Uig Crofters Ltd.	Uig Crofters (Lewis)	46,300
Maj. John & Capt. A. Wills	Applecross	45,700
Lord Thorneycroft	Eishkin (Lewis)	43,900
Barvas Ests. Ltd.	Barvas (Lewis)	41,900
M. H. & F. H. D. H. Wills	Torran etc.	37,400
Ian MacPherson	Attadale	35,700
Benmore Ests.	Benmore	35,200
A. S., A. F. & M. M. Roger	Dundonell	32,700
Miss E. J. M. Douglas	Kililian	31,500
J. F. Robinson	Morsgail (Lewis)	31,400
Lochluichart Ests. Ltd.	Kinlochluichart	28,700
A. B. L. Munro Ferguson	Novar	28,700
Carloway Ests. Ltd.	Carloway (Lewis)	26,600
Maj. I. M. Scobie	Rhidderoch	24,200
Lady McCorquodale	Gruinard	24,300
R. Williams	Strathvaich	23,000
A. Carlton Greg	Loch Carron	23,000
Park Crofters Ests. Ltd.	Park Crofters (Lewis)	23,000
Mrs Barker, Mrs Kershaw	Soval (Lewis)	22,800
Lord Burton	Dochfour	20,000
Exc. of Vt. Mountgarret	Wyvis	19,800
Vt. Portman	Inverinate	19,400
Maj. & Mrs Braithwaite	Ben Damph	18,800
A. M. Hickey	Glencalvie	18,800
Grimerston Ests. Ltd.	Grimerston (Lewis)	18,800
T. W. Sandiman	Fannich	18,700
Muriel Calder	Braemore	18,700
Dorothy A. Balcan	Aultbea	18,500
C. S. R. Stroyan	Monar	18,500
Mr MacDonald	Inverasdale	18,200
Lt. Col. J. D. Hignett	Kildermorie	17,000
Dr S. M. Whitteridge	Inverlael	15,900
The Polly Est. Ltd.	Inverpolly	15,300
John Wills	Grudie	14,800
A. I. Sladen	Glen Carron	14,800
L. W. Robson	Inverbran	14,400
Maj. J. P. Harrington	Strathrusdale	14,100
K. MacKenzie	Aline	13,500
P. Wilson	Loch Rosque	13,200
P. S. Henman	Benmore, Coigach	12,600
I. S. Smilie	Langwell Lodge	12,600
Sir J. Brooke Bt.	Midfearn	12,600
Unknown	W. Benula	12,300
G. & B. H. C. Van veen	E. Rhidderoch	12,200
E. H. Vestey	Assynt	11,700
Lewis Crofters Ltd.	Lewis Crofters (Lewis)	11,200
The Corriemulzie Est.	Corriemulzie	10,800
Hon. P. J. W. Fairfax	E. Benula	10,700
Sir John Stirling	Fairburn	9,900

Unknown	Luberoy	9,800
Unknown	Wastenly, Arbol	9,500
H. & R. Combe	Scandroy	9,400
Marq. de Torrehermes	Starban	9,100
Chairman Langstaff	Badentarbet	9,000
Gairloch Sands Holiday Centre	Big Sands	9,000
Unknown	Corriehallie	7,200
Com. C. G. Tyner	Strathkinnaird	6,700
C. M. Beatie	Leckhelm	6,700
G. S. Richardson	Gladfield	6,700
Unknown	N. Cluaine	6,700
G. Girvan	Corrieclair	6,700
Col. A. D. Vickers	Tulloch	6,300
Maj. Botley, Maj. Don	Arnacraig	6,300
Tr. of Lord Seaforth	Brahan	5,800
J. D. Laurie	Little Gruinard	5,700
Mrs Dunphie	Eilea Darroch	5,500
Eagle Star Ins. Co.	Rosehaugh, Kilcoy	5,500

Totals of Estates down to 5,000 acres

73 Estates — 1,578,300 acres

Estates 5,000 to 1,000 acres

Between	5,000 and 4,000 acres:	1:	4,000 acres
	4,000 and 3,000 acres:	8:	27,700 acres
	3,000 and 2,000 acres:	13:	31,000 acres
	2,000 and 1,000 acres:	18:	23,800 acres

Totals of Estates 5,000 to 1,000 acres

40 Estates — 86,500 acres

Summary

Estates between	75,000 and 50,000 acres:	6:	379,400 acres
	50,000 and 40,000 acres:	4:	177,800 acres
	40,000 and 30,000 acres:	6:	203,900 acres
	30,000 and 20,000 acres:	10:	244,300 acres
	20,000 and 10,000 acres:	28:	427,900 acres
	10,000 and 5,000 acres:	18:	134,800 acres
	5,000 and 1,000 acres:	40:	86,500 acres

Total of Estates down to 1,000 acres

102 Estates — 1,654,600 acres

Total land area of county ....1,997,254 acres

Total area of private Estates down to 1,000 acres ....1,654,600 acres

INVERNESS

With its huge area of 2,695,094 acres, this is the largest county in Scotland — I thought in Great Britain but Yorkshire beats it by a cool 1,181,800 acres (Note, the 00's are actual).

However, when anyone tries to cover it, as Millman did in the field and I did on his maps, it is, in all conscience, big enough. Like Ross, it was, in 1874, crammed with huge estates. There are not now so many over 100,000 acres. The largest owner then was Lovat (Fraser family) with 162,000 acres (£28,200). As far as I can make out, the acreage of this estate today is 76,000, but it is stated in other records to be 190,000 acres, an increase of 28,000 acres since 1874. Quite recently I wrote to the estate office asking if they could confirm that this huge area belongs to Lord Lovat still. I got no reply. In any event 76,000 acres is surely big enough, but the Lovats have not been easily satisfied. At the time of the build-up of electricity by the North of Scotland Hydro Electric Board, a short stretch of the lord's salmon river was affected, for which £100,000 compensation was paid. Press reports stated that when his fellow landlords were chivvying him about getting double that amount, he regretted that he had not got the £200,000, which increased figure would have suited him very well.

The Lovats are famed, but so are the Seafields who, in Inverness, owned 160,000 acres, but, in total, including Banff and Moray, reached 305,700 acres with an annual value of £72,600. By 1970 the extent of Seafield's land is 185,200 acres (Inverness 86,600 acres). The Seafields continue to be one of the largest owners in Scotland, although the present owner has quite recently been selling large areas, so he must, at last, be feeling the pinch.

There were in 1874, another seven owners of over 100,000 acres, I shall mention the following:

Baillie, Dochfour had 141,000 acres but is now reduced (in this county) to around 20,000 acres.

Cameron of Lochiel's 110,000 acres is not much reduced now at 97,000 acres — a figure he confirmed recently on television.

MacDonald of Armadale, Skye had in 1874, 130,000 acres and now has only 41,700.

MacLeod of Dunvegan has dropped from 142,000 to 34,500 acres.

The remarkable thing about the last three names is that in 1895 they all appeared to give evidence to the 'Red Deer Commission'. On this commission was a Socialist minister of the Free Church who was always ready, when these big wigs appeared in the witness box, to tackle them severely. His questions and remarks reduced them to their true size and value as Scottish citizens.

Lovat also was called as a witness, but sent a representative who told how, as land was improved by a crofter or cottar, the laird took possession and moved the worker on to reclaim another small area. MacCallum (the aforementioned clergyman) elicited this by his questioning. MacCallum of Muckairn's name was a household word in the Highlands when I was young.

This 1895 Commission report, now unobtainable, should be unearthed. If anyone can put me on to a copy for sale, please let me know.

Much more could be written about landlordism in this huge county.

Someone might like to examine the way in which Hereward Wake's 62,000 estate in Harris was sold, and more recently the actual owners of "Uig Crofters Ltd." estate of 46,300 acres in Lewis.

INVERNESS

Land area	Mainland	1,916,768	2,695,094 acres
	Islands	778,326	
Inland water	Mainland	67,399	97,397 acres
	Islands	29,998	

Estates down to 5,000 acres

Owner	Estates	Acres
British Aluminium Co. Ltd.	British Aluminium Ests.	103,200
Sir D. Cameron	Lochiel Ests.	97,600
S. Uist Ests. Ltd.	S. Uist & Islands	92,200
Countess of Seafield	Seafield Ests.	86,600
Lord Lovat	Lovat Ests.	76,000
Maj. Hereward Wake	Amnhuinnsuidhe (Harris)	62,500
Lord Dulverton (Wills)	Glenfeshie, Fassifern	52,700
N. Uist & Benbecula Ests.	N. Uist & Islands	50,000
Sir Oliver Crosswaithe-Eyre	Knoydart	43,000
Sir W. P. Ramsden	Ardverikie	42,900
Lord MacDonald	Sleat Ests.	41,700
John MacLeod of MacLeod	Dunvegan	34,500
Wm. Gordon of Lude	Arrisdale	27,700
Capt. Sandison	Glentromie	27,000
M. J. Beecher	Arisaig	22,500
Taylor Bros.	Abernethy	22,000
Th. Girvan	W. Ceannacroc	21,500
M. N. C. Ford	Meoble	21,300
John Cameron	Balmacaan	20,000
J. P. Grant	Rothiemurchus	19,800
Unknown	Stocknish	19,500
P. H. Byam Cook	Ben Alder	18,900

Lord Burton	Dochfour	18,300
Robert Ellice	Glenfarrar	18,000
Glendale Crofters Ltd.	Glendale Crofters (Skye)	18,000
The MacNeil	Barra & Islands	17,200
W. MacKenzie Goodman	Glendoe	17,100
J. C. & P. Wilson	Garrogie	17,000
Mrs E. Findlay	S. Drumochter	16,900
R. J. & A. Trapp Ltd.	Braeroy	16,700
D. Cameron	Glen Nevis	16,300
Tr. Late D. I. C. MacLean	Clune & Cluny	16,200
J. L. MacDonald	Skebost (Skye)	16,200
M. A. Johnston	Strathaird (Skye)	15,000
Hon. P. M. Samuel	Phoine, Etteridge	14,400
J. M. Grant	Glen Morriston	14,000
D. R. MacDonald	Waternish (Skye)	13,100
Sir J. Fuller	Cozac	12,300
Nether Pollok (Maxwell)	Bheinn Bhine Deer Forest	12,200
Mr Hayward	Newtonmore	12,200
Mrs L. P. Cameron-Head	Inverailort	11,600
Sir J. Barber	Drumnaglass	10,800
Maj. Gen. MacDonald	Braes (Skye)	10,700
Unknown	Dalraddy	10,600
A. G. Forbes Leith	Dunachton	10,400
Sligachan Hotel	Sligachan	10,200
J. C. Cremer	Pitmain	9,900
G. M. T. Pretyman	Corrygarth	9,500
Col. Eliot Holt	Corryborough	9,500
Mrs Wilkie Griss	Guisachan	9,000
Brig. Kewley	N. Drumochter	9,000
Lord Bilsland	Kinrara	9,000
T. E. MacLeod Hilleary	Edinbane, Lyndale (Skye)	9,000
Lord Elphinstone	Glen Mazeran	8,300
Westminster (Liverpool) Tr. Co. Ltd.	Dorlin	8,100
Unknown	Culligram	7,700
Earl Bradford	Dell	7,600
Moray Estates Dev. Co.	Castle Stuart	7,600
Wm. I. Bruges	Tulloch House	7,600
Mr & Mrs J. Lees-Millais	Glenmoidart	7,600
A. McKellaig	Glenfinnan	7,200
R. Morrison, H. Evans	Eigg (Isle)	7,000
A. Spencer Nairn	Struy	6,700
Lewis Briggs	Cullachy	6,700
F. T. Davies	Aberarder	6,600
Unknown	Glenspean	6,400
G. Forbes	Balayil	6,300
Lt. Com. L. R. D. MacKintosh of MacKintosh	Moymore	6,200
D. J. Wilson	Moy	6,000
H. Birkbeck	Kinlochourn	6,000
Unknown	Vallay (N. Uist)	6,000
E. D. H. MacRae	Clava	5,600
A. Dunbar	Inverarne	5,400
Tr. A. D. R. Walker	Achlain	5,400
Unknown	Dalnagarvie	5,400
Gen. Martin	Husabost (Skye)	5,300
Tr. T. H. Hatford	Scalpay	5,200
Mr MacDonald	Strathconnan	5,100
Eagle Star Ins. Co.	Knockie Lodge	5,000
Col. R. Swire	Arbost (Skye)	5,000

Totals of Estates down to 5,000 acres

80 Estates — 1,586,800 acres

Estates 5,000 to 1,000 acres

Estates between			
5,000 and 4,000 acres:	9:	40,000 acres
4,000 and 3,000 acres:	13:	45,300 acres
3,000 and 2,000 acres:	21:	50,900 acres
2,000 and 1,000 acres:	18:	25,300 acres

Totals of Estates 5,000 to 1,000 acres

61 Estates — 161,500 acres

Summary

Estates over	100,000 acres:		1:	103,200 acres
Estates between	100,000 and 75,000 acres:	4:	352,400 acres
	75,000 and 50,000 acres:	3:	165,200 acres
	50,000 and 40,000 acres:	3:	127,600 acres
	40,000 and 30,000 acres:	1:	34,500 acres
	30,000 and 20,000 acres:	7:	162,400 acres
	20,000 and 10,000 acres:	27:	403,600 acres
	10,000 and 5,000 acres:	34:	237,900 acres
	5,000 and 1,000 acres:	61:	161,500 acres

Grand total of Estates down to 1,000 acres

141 Estates — 1,748,300 acres

Total land area of county ....2,695,094 acres

Total area of private Estates down to 1,000 acres ....1,748,300 acres

ARGYLL

This sure is Campbell country, and it was particularly so in 1874. The Duke owned 163,315 acres (£45,672). His relative the Earl of Breadalbane had more land — 179,225 acres — but of half the value (£21,165). The 50-strong host of other Campbells held 424,000 acres (£57,000) making a clean total of 766,500 acres worth annually £123,800.

Argyll, with its two million acres, is a huge county, but the Campbells accounted for a big chunk of it.

Today the position is drastically changed, with the Duke holding a mere 73,400 acres, and two other Campbells, MacKie Campbell of

Stonefield with 9,000 acres and I. N. Campbell of Cumlodden with 7,200 making the family total 89,600 acres. And now the poor Duke of Argyll has to go the world over to find money to keep a roof over his head in his Inveraray Castle. Changed days, but not changed nearly enough.

Argyll, nowadays, is the most forward-looking of the Crofting Counties. It is certainly more broken-up, as seen by the 1970 lists of owners, but, apart from that, it was the first county in Scotland to be able to boast, in 1961-62, that the Forestry Commission, in its State-owned forest, had reached the 100,000 acres stage.

Today there are no private estates over 100,000 acres in Argyll, but there are still those, such as the Morrisons — the Islay whisky producers — with 74,400 acres, and the Duke with his 73,400 acres amongst the bunch.

Of eleven who own estates down to 20,000 acres, many new names appear, including the Noble family at Glenkinglass. Lord Kinglass declared, when Willie Ross established the Highlands and Islands Development Board, that we were going completely communist.

Adjoining the Nobles are the Flemings (of Dundee) who are big London finance merchants, and their relative, Lady Wyfold — between them owning almost 100,000 acres.

In Mull we have the reactionary Masserene family adjoining the Glenforsa estate, acquired by the State many years ago to be used as a demonstration farm. It had been hoped that this excellent land could be used to prove the terrific potential for food production of such areas. Damage caused by red deer was heart breaking.

In 1974 Mr (now Lord) Campbell, the Tory Secretary of State was on the point of selling Glenforsa back to the sporting gentry. Willie Ross was just in time to stop this. A survey of the land, and recommendations for its use were made. These have now been implemented by the H.I.D.B. by having the estate broken up into two farms of 5,000 acres each, let out to individual farmers, and 2,600 acres handed over to the Forestry Commission. I feel St Andrews House showed lack of vision here. Why on earth should the resources of the Department of Fisheries and Food (as the Department of Agriculture is now called) and the world-renowned Hill Farming Organisation, with brilliant men like Dr Cunningham, not be used to make a success of Glenforsa?

The recent acquistion by the H.I.D.B. on the mainland opposite Mull of almost 4,000 acres of hill land (at £75 per acre) to be used as a demonstration farm for red deer production may be psychologically sound.

Argyll could have masses more written about it. It should be noted that there are great extremes of land quality — e.g. between Blackmount and the fertile lands of Kintyre.

ARGYLL

Land area	Mainland	1,469,445	1,990,522 acres
	Islands	521,077	
Inland water	Mainland	27,623	35,357 acres
	Islands	7,734	

Estates down to 5,000 acres

Owner	Estate	Acres
Islay Estates Ltd.	Islay Est.	74,400
Duke of Argyll	Argyll Est	73,400
R. Fleming	Blackmount	51,000
Lady Wyfold	Glen Kinglass	41,200
Jura Ltd. (Astor)	Tarbert (Jura)	41,100
Ardtornish Est. Ltd.	Ardtornish	34,400
J. M. Guthrie	Conaglen	31,000
Noble Family	Ardkinglass	30,500
Mrs A. R. Nelson	Ardlussa (Jura)	22,000
Miss C. MacLean	Ardgour	20,700
Mrs Faller-Bell	Dalness	20,600
Viscountess Masserene	Knock (Mull)	18,700
Bruno L. Schroder	Dunlossit (Jura)	17,700
J. T. Thomas	Ardnamurchan	17,100
R. Campbell Preston	Ardchattan	16,200
Craignure Est. Ltd.	Torosay (Mull)	15,500
Western Heritable Inv. Ltd.	Kintour (Islay)	15,300
Unknown	Loch Buie (Mull)	14,900
Tr. C. A. M. Oates	Skipness	14,700
Sir L. T. Lithgow	Ormsary	14,400
J. Maxwell MacDonald	Largie	14,400
Maj. O. B. Clapham	Laggan (Islay)	14,300
Hon. Mr Dalness	Altnafeadh	13,100
Arthur Strutt	Kingairloch	12,600
C. K. M. Stewart	Coll (Isle)	12,300
F. A. Riley Smith	Ardfin (Jura)	11,900
Simon Fraser	Glenure	11,500
R. M. Abel-Smith	Laudale	11,300
M. W. Brand Aitken	Auch	11,200
Lt. Col. & Mrs Nicholl	Black Corries	10,800
Fenton Barns (N. Berwick)	Ardlarig	10,800
Rt. Hon. Lord Strachcona	Colonsay (Isle)	10,500
V. P. Hardwick	Pennyghael (Mull)	10,400
H. M. Speirs	Glenborrodale	10,300
R. M. Malcolm	Poltalloch	9,500

D. H. Rogers	Ellary	9,000
Mackie Campbell	Stonefield	9,000
Unknown	Killean Lodge	7,900
Atlas Investment Co.	Castles	7,700
A. C. Farquharson	Torloisk (Mull)	7,700
Mrs H. Sassoon	BenBuie (Mull)	7,300
Tr. of late Holman	Acharacle	7,200
Sir I. M. Campbell	Cumlodden	7,200
Fitzroy MacLean	Strachur	7,200
The Chalmers Property (Holman)	Killiechronan	7,000
Schuster & others	Duiletter	6,900
Unknown	Glenlonan	6,800
Unknown	Ederline	6,800
Mrs V. I. Montgomery	Kinnabus (Islay)	6,800
British Aluminium Co. Ltd.	British Aluminium	6,300
R. M. B. McAllister	Glenbarr	6,300
G. R. Rickman & M. S. Wilson	Leanganbeach (Jura)	6,000
Sir W. J. Lithgow	Inver (Jura)	6,000
Mrs Pollok	Ronachan	5,900
John McPherson	Ballimeanach	5,500
C. S. Bailey	Inversanda	5,400
Brig. R. W. L. Fellowes	Cladich	5,400
J. H. C. Crerar	Breckley	5,400
Unknown	Knockdow	5,400
Economic Forestry Group	Ballochyle	5,400
Tr. of late J. MacRae Gilstrap	Ballimore	5,400
Tr. of Wailbrook	Carskiey	5,400
A. B. MacArthur	Arnicle	5,200
Hugh MacPhail	Achnashinch	5,100
H. I. MacDonald	Barguillean	5,100
Mrs Billimeir	Melfort	5,000
A. Colville	Rahoy	5,000

Totals of Estates down to 5,000 acres

67 Estates — 963,400 acres

Estates 5,000 to 1,000 acres

Between			
	5,000 and 4,000 acres:	17:	74,300 acres
	4,000 and 3,000 acres:	18:	61,900 acres
	3,000 and 2,000 acres:	35:	82,200 acres
	2,000 and 1,000 acres:	47:	60,000 acres

Totals of Estates 5,000 to 1,000 acres

117 Estates — 278,700 acres

Summary

Estates between			
	75,000 and 50,000 acres:	3:	198,800 acres
	50,000 and 40,000 acres:	2:	82,300 acres
	40,000 and 30,000 acres:	3:	95,900 acres
	30,000 and 20,000 acres:	3:	63,300 acres
	20,000 and 10,000 acres:	23:	309,900 acres
	10,000 and 5,000 acres:	33:	213,200 acres
	5,000 and 1,000 acres:	117:	278,700 acres

Grand total Estates down to 1,000 acres

184 Estates — 1,242,100 acres

Total of land area of county...............................1,990,522 acres

Total area of private Estates down to 1,000 acres ....1,242,100 acres

BUTE

This small county of 140,000 acres is made up of a collection of islands: Bute itself, the two Cumbraes and Arran. It has recently been officially taken into the family of Crofting Counties, and thus comes into our West area.

Here again are extremes of land quality, the flat fertile land of Bute as compared with the quite mountainous parts of Arran.

Bute and the Cumbraes are entirely owned by the Marquis of Bute. In 1874 the Marquis had 29,300 acres, and today 25,000 acres (in this county).

The Duke of Hamilton used to have Brodick Castle estate with 102,200 acres (£18,700) here, which has now gone from his family, but he still owns 5,200 acres in East Lothian.

BUTE

Land area	139,711 acres
Inland water	805 acres

Estates down to 5,000 acres

Owner	Estates	Acres
Arran Estate	Arran Ests.	29,000
The Lady Mary Boscawan	Dougne	27,400
Marquess of Bute	Bute Ests.	25,100
Nat. trust for Scotland	Brodick Castle	6,500

Totals of Estates down to 5,000 acres

4 Estates — 88,000 acres

Estates of 5,000 to 1,000 acres

Between			
	4,000 and 3,000 acres:	1:	3,200 acres
	2,000 and 1,000 acres:	7:	9,000 acres

Totals of Estates 5,000 to 1,000 acres

8 Estates — 12,200 acres

Summary

Estates between   30,000 and 20,000 acres: 3:   81,500 acres
                            10,000 and 5,000 acres: 1:   6,500 acres
                             5,000 and 1,000 acres: 8:   12,200 acres

Grand total of Estates down to 1,000 acres

12 Estates — 100,200 acres

Total land area of county .... 139,711 acres

Total land area of private Estates down to 1,000 acres ....   100,200 acres

Summary of Estates down to 1,000 acres in the

Five Crofting Counties plus Bute

In Thousands

COUNTY	100+ Est.	Acres	100/75 Est.	Acres	75/50 Est.	Acres	50/40 Est.	Acres	40/30 Est.	Acres	30/20 Est.	Acres	20/10 Est.	Acres	10/5 Est.	Acres	5/1 Est.	Acres
CAITHNESS	—	—	1	81.4	1	52.6	1	48.0	1	33.8	1	27.5	7	100.8	6	41.4	17	46.1
SUTHERLAND	2	236.2	—	—	2	122.3	3	124.1	4	145.1	6	145.9	10	166.0	10	73.1	15	45.4
ROSS AND CROMARTY	—	—	—	—	6	379.4	4	177.8	6	203.9	10	244.3	28	427.9	18	134.8	40	86.5
INVERNESS	1	103.2	4	352.4	3	165.2	3	127.6	1	34.5	7	162.4	27	403.6	34	237.9	61	161.5
ARGYLL	—	—	—	—	3	198.8	2	82.3	3	95.9	3	63.3	23	309.9	33	213.2	117	278.7
BUTE	—	—	—	—	—	—	—	—	—	—	3	81.5	—	—	1	6.5	8	12.2
TOTALS	3	339.4	5	433.8	15	918.3	13	559.8	15	513.2	30	643.4	95	1408.2	102	706.9	258	630.4

NORTH-EAST (NE)

This region has 7 counties from Nairn to Angus and Perth, and there are 609 private estates down to 1,000 acres with 3,424,300 acres.

Nairn
Moray
Banff
Aberdeen
Kincardine
Angus
Perthshire

The North East plus Perthshire

NAIRN

We are now into very different land from that in the West, but landownership remains more or less the same.

This is one of our smallest counties, just 104,252 acres, much less than many estates in the West. Still, it has its big owners, such as Lord Cawdor (a Campbell) of Cawdor Castle. In 1874 he owned 46,200 acres — almost half the county. This Campbell has held onto his land more cleverly than those in Argyll, and may in fact still own 46,000 acres, though Millman's maps record only 38,300. This landlord also owns land in Inverness, and since the recent (1970s) break-up of the Seafield estates, Cawdor seems to be purchasing their land in a big way. The only other big owner is Brodie of Lethen, in 1874 22,400 acres, now 16,000 acres.

The Earl of Leven and Melville's estate Glenferness, has dropped from 7,800 to 5,500 acres, but he also owns much land in the South.

This county is now included in the Five Crofting Counties under H.I.D.B., perhaps fortunately, but I cannot see why. I know this corner intimately and would associate Moray and Nairn as twin counties, no crofting in either county that I know of.

The Wills family, with huge holdings in the West, now appear in the North East with land, about 4,000 acres at Culmony.

NAIRN

Land area	104,252 acres
Inland water	760 acres

Estates down to 5,000 acres

Owner	Estates	Acres
Earl of Cawdor (Campbell)	Cawdor	38,300
Tr. of D. J. Brodie	Lethen	15,900
Earl of Leven & Melville	Glenferness	5,500

42

Totals of Estates down to 5,000 acres

3 Estates — 59,700 acres

Estates 5,000 to 1,000 acres

Between

5,000 and 4,000 acres:	1:	4,000 acres
4,000 and 3,000 acres:	1:	3,300 acres
3,000 and 2,000 acres:	2:	5,500 acres
2,000 and 1,000 acres:	4:	4,300 acres

Totals of Estates 5,000 to 1,000 acres

8 Estates — 17,100 acres

Summary

Estates between

40,000 and 30,000 acres:	1:	38,300 acres
20,000 and 10,000 acres:	1:	15,900 acres
10,000 and 5,000 acres:	1:	5,500 acres
5,000 and 1,000 acres:	8:	17,100 acres

Grand total of private Estates down to 1,000 acres

11 Estates — 76,800 acres

Total of land area of county .... 104,252 acres

Total area of private Estates down to 1,000 acres .... 76,800 acres

MORAY

This county I know intimately. I worked for one year on Altyre estate, and another eight years pioneering with the Forestry Commission at Monaughty and Teindland forests in the 1920s. It is a delightful county.

Three of the big owners in 1874 still hold large areas, but Seafield comes down from 97,000 to 57,000 acres, while Moray Estates go up from 22,000 to 24,000 acres. Altyre, belonging to the Gordon Cummings takes a big knock from 36,400 to 12,500 acres.

I was on Altyre as a working forester in 1907/8. The laird then had married a rich American, and, besides spending a lot of money on fancy stabling, did not quite overlook the workers. A really first class foresters' bothy was built. But Gordon Cummings got into trouble, and working staff was reduced (and the stables emptied). I cannot forget two weeks of gruelling work in a blazing July sun on their extensive grouse moors, slaving with a pick, shovelling, wheelbarrowing, and spreading gravel to make service roads for

43

gamekeepers and 'the toffs' to use on August 12th. I took ill and lay alone for a couple of days in an improvised bothy on this bare moorland. My two co-workers were out all the time.

Two Dukes of this county have lost land here, The Duke of Fife dropping from 41,000 acres to 'no mention', and the Duke of Richmond and Gordon similarly from 12,000 acres, in the 1970 survey.

Two newcomers, now to be found all over Scotland have appeared, the Eagle Star Insurance Co. with 18,000 and the Wills family with 8,200 acres.

Can we afford to allow such playing around to go on with our land of such high quality?

MORAY

Land area	304,931 acres
Inland water	3,198 acres

Estates down to 5,000 acres

Owner	Estate	Acres
Earl of Seafield	Seafield Estates	57,500
Earl of Moray	Moray Estates	23,900
Eagle Star Ins. Co.	Rothes & Craigellachie	17,900
Sir William Gordon Cumming	Altyre	12,500
A. Grant Laing	Relugas-Dunphail	10,600
Dallas Est. P. Strutt & Walker	Dallas	10,500
Tr. H. D. H. Wills	Pluscarden, Knockando	8,200
Lady MacPherson Grant	Ballindalloch	8,000
Ian H. Tennant	Innes House	6,300
Tr. J. Brander Dunbar	Pitgaveny	5,000

Totals of Estates down to 5,000 acres

10 Estates — 160,400 acres

Estates 5,000 to 1,000 acres

Between			
5,000 acres and 4,000 acres:	1:	4,000 acres
4,000 acres and 3,000 acres:	4:	12,600 acres
3,000 acres and 2,000 acres:	6:	13,900 acres
2,000 acres and 1,000 acres:	9:	13,000 acres

Totals of Estates 5,000 to 1,000 acres

20 Estates — 43,500 acres

Summary

Estates between			
75,000 and 50,000 acres:	1:	57,500 acres
30,000 and 20,000 acres;	1:	23,900 acres
20,000 and 10,000 acres:	4:	51,500 acres
10,000 and 5,000 acres:	4:	27,500 acres
5,000 and 1,000 acres:	20:	43,500 acres

44

Grand total of Estates down to 1,000 acres

30 Estates — 203,900 acres

Total land area of county .... 304,931 acres

Total area of private Estates down to 1,000 acres .... 203,900 acres

BANFF

Another small county with much rich, fertile land. The Seafield Estate still retains a huge area (41,000) of this along the coast. This was my first training ground — at Cullen House. As foresters, we were the estates' drudges at the beck and call of all the other estate departments: game keepers, home farm etc. and reached an annual climax in a solid week's beating of filthy carpets after one year's constant treading in the 'big Hoose'. It was dreadful work. The Seafields can now find no use for this white elephant of 365 windows.

Three big owners have disappeared as far as my lists go from this county — again, the Dukes of Fife and of Richmond and Gordon, and also Major Gordon Duff.

But I had experience of the Duke of Richmond and Gordon's presence in the 1920s. When the Forestry Commission bought 1,100 acres from him in 1923, he retained the shooting rights. I was given charge of the planting of this area. Game was, and is, the forester's biggest problem, red deer, roe deer, hares, rabbits (not 'game', but preserved), grouse and black game. I had to get the work done as efficiently and as cheaply as possible, so I reduced fencing to a minimum and employed a selected man to control rabbits, hares, and in the case of Teindland, roe deer. This trapper was so successful that we did not erect a single yard of fencing. He belonged to a local family, had gone to Canada as a youth but returned in 1914 to join the army and got badly smashed. When I employed him he was married with two of a family. He may — I was not aware of this — have taken the odd grouse or pheasant. In any case, two keepers did catch him shooting a pheasant (which they were never able to produce). This serious game offence was reported to the estate factor. I was ordered by the Forestry Commission to get rid of Davy at once and the estate would push him out of his house. I refused to comply. In an interview, the factor agreed that if the shooting tenant (the 'shoot' was let out by the estate to a Glasgow business man in

45

Aberlour) agreed to overlook the matter, the estate would. The tenant (Mr Findlay) willingly did so, but the Duke would not have it at any price. Davy was taken to court in Banff (where he was fined 10/-) and came back to work with the Forestry Commission, but not with a gun, just as an ordinary squad worker. Such are the ways of our arrogant 'upper ten', and the factor is not always to blame. That Duke, the factor, Davy and the Forestry Commission officers-in-charge are all gone. The present Duke owns less land and even has to earn his living. This should happen, and will, to all landlords, in time.

The Wills family have a huge acquisition (34,000 acres) at Glenavon, and another newcomer, Major H. S. Cayzer owns 10,000 acres in the Cabrach.

BANFF

Land area	403,054 acres
Inland water	1,977 acres

Estates down to 5,000 acres

Owner	Estate	Acres
Earl of Seafield	Seafield Estate	41,100
David S. Wills	Glenavon	33,900
Feued Farms	Keith (Newmill)	13,100
Exc. Sir G. MacPherson Grant	Ballindalloch	13,000
Maj. H. J. Morton	Glenfiddich	11,100
Maj. H. S. Cayzer	Cabrach	10,000
Alex Garden	Troup	9,900
Tr. of Miss Cowie and Mrs Cuming	Glenrinnes	9,100
Unknown	Drummuir	6,500
Tr. Sir G. Abercromby	Forglen	6,400

Totals of Estates down to 5,000 acres

10 Estates — 154,100 acres

Estates 5,000 to 1,000 acres

Between			
5,000 and 4,000 acres:	5:	21,800 acres
4,000 and 3,000 acres:	6:	21,300 acres
3,000 and 2,000: acres	5:	11,800 acres
2,000 and 1,000 acres:	13:	18,000 acres

Totals of Estates 5,000 to 1,000 acres

29 Estates — 72,900 acres

Summary

Estates between			
50,000 and 40,000 acres:	1:	41,100 acres
40,000 and 30,000 acres:	1:	33,900 acres

46

20,000 and 10,000 acres:	4:	47,200 acres
10,000 and 5,000 acres:	4:	31,900 acres
5,000 and 1,000 acres:	29:	72,900 acres

Grand total of Estates down to 1,000 acres

39 Estates— 227,000 acres

Total land area of county .... 403,054 acres

Total area of private Estates down to 1,000 acres .... 227,000 acres

ABERDEEN

Again, there are big changes in ownership in the last century, but in a county of 1¼ million acres, these somehow do not seem so desperate.

The fortunes of the Dukes of Fife and of Richmond and Gordon declined in this county as they did in Moray and Banff. The really big name in 1874 was Farquharson of Invercauld with 87,700 acres (£9,567) and this estate is still 75,000 acres. It is said to be much larger, but I cannot trace any more of it. Farquharson, however, owns much land also in Perthshire and Argyll, and is today not far behind Buccleuch.

The Gordons, like the Campbells in Argyll, seem to have had a family tradition of landownership.There were 28 of them in 1874, including, at Cluny Castle (20,000), the successor of the infamous Col. Gordon of Cluny who in 1841 had bought Barra, South Uist and Benbecula and perpetrated there cruelties equal to those of the Sutherlands in Strathnaver, as related in Hunter's *The Crofting Community,* 1976. Only one Gordon appears by name in the over 5,000 list today (Knockespock).

The Marquis of Huntly owned 8,000 acres in 1874 but does not appear in Millman's lists — at least under that name.

There are three estates for which I have not been able to ascertain an owner. (There is a certain coyness about claiming ownership these days).

Royalty, in the person of Queen Victoria was credited in 1874 with 25,350 acres (£2,392). Now, our Queen Elizabeth II has, in Aberdeen, increased this to almost 29,000 acres, with more in Angus.

Viscount Cowdray does not appear in 1874, but now owns 65,500 acres here plus 21,600 in Kincardine, where he nearly bounds with his relative the Duke of Atholl. But why should we deny the so-called wealthiest man in Britain access to lands in Scotland? Personally, I would as soon have him as a laird as the Duke of Atholl with his private army, but, I keep repeating, I hope it does not last much longer.

ABERDEEN

Land area		1,261,333 acres
Inland water		6,970 acres

Estates down to 5,000 acres

Owner	*Estates*	*Acres*
Capt. A. A. C. Farquharson	Invercauld	75,000
Vt. Cowdray	Dunecht Estate	65,600
Harlay & Jones (Invests.) Ltd.	Mar Lodge	51,200
The Queen	Balmoral	28,900
Tr. Late Lord Glentanar	Glentanar	26,900
Fyvie Settlement Trust (alias A. G. Forbes)	Fyvie Estate	24,400
Rattray Discretionary Trust	Haddo-Rattray	24,200
Capt. A. A. Ramsay	Mar	23,000
Stewart's Estates Aberdeen Ltd.	Slains Castle	23,000
The MacRobert Trust	Dounside	19,000
Property Realisation Ltd.	Strichen	15,000
Mrs A. M. Farquharson	Finzean	14,700
Trustees of the Late A. Wallace	Candacraig	13,900
Unknown	Huntly Castle	12,300
Sir C. H. Barclay-Harvey	Dinnet (Kinnaird)	12,000
Lady Doris Duff	Hatton	11,300
P. Strachan	Edingarrioch	10,800
Col. Sir I. P. A. M. Walker-Okeover Bt.	Glenmuick	10,200
J. H. Seton Gordon	Abergeldie	10,200
Tr. of Late A. & F. P. Morrison	Bogney	10,000
Unknown	Fetterangus	10,000
Aboyne Trust	Dinnet (A. Tr.)	9,500
H. Q. Forbes Irvine	Drum	9,200
Bridges InterVivos Trust	Bonnykelly	8,000
G. S. Barnett Stuart	Dens, Crichie	8,000
The Hon. G. Astor	Tullydromie, Deskry	8,000
Unknown	Logie Grimond	7,400
Tr. Sir A. MacLean	Littlewood	7,000
Udny & Dudwick Ests. Ltd.	Udny	7,000
James Stott	Crichie	6,900
Unknown	Blyth Estate	6,800
Kilmundy Est. Ltd.	Kilmundy	6,400
Lt. R. S. Gordon	Knockespock	6,100
Unknown	Drummossie	5,800
Unknown	Killermony	5,800
Unknown	Balthogie	5,400
Nigel I. Forbes	Castle Forbes	5,400

Alex B. Moir	Cairness	5,000
J. H. Ingleby & others	Blairmore	5,000
Williamston Ests. Ltd.	Williamston	5,000
Jas. C. Moir	Tulloch	5,000
Ellon Castle Estates	Ellon Castle	5,000
Tr. Lady Louise Stockdale	Delnadamph	5,000
Aboyne & Densmuir Estates	Aboyne	5,000

Totals of Estates down to 5,000 acres

44 Estates — 639,300 acres

Estates 5,000 to 1,000 acres

Between	5,000 and 4,000 acres:	12:	53,200 acres
	4,000 and 3,000 acres:	33:	110,800 acres
	3,000 and 2,000 acres:	32:	75,000 acres
	2,000 and 1,000 acres:	33:	48,300 acres

Total of Estates 5,000 to 1,000 acres

110 Estates — 287,300 acres

Summary

Estates between	100,000 and 75,000 acres:	1: 75,000 acres
	75,000 and 50,000 acres:	2: 116,800 acres
	30,000 and 20,000 acres:	6: 150,400 acres
	20,000 and 10,000 acres:	12: 149,400 acres
	10,000 and 5,000 acres:	23: 147,700 acres
	5,000 and 1,000 acres:	110: 287,300 acres

Grand total of Estates down to 1,000 acres

154 Estates — 926,600 acres

Total land area of County ....1,261,333 acres

Total area of private Estates down to 1,000 acres .... 926,600 acres

---

KINCARDINE

Another small county — yet in 1874 there was one large estate, Fasque House, belonging to the family of the 'axe man', Prime Minister Gladstone (so called for his interest in timber). The acreage was then 45,062 (£9,174). The Gladstones seem to know what they are doing, as they now own 47,700 acres. Their forestry is in fact reasonably good.

Again, several largish estates have disappeared — or do not now show up e.g. Arbuthnot, Crathes and Durno. I guess that Cowdray of Dunecht has mopped up some of this, with his 21,600 acres in this county. The Arbuthnots, I should think, continue to be the best-known family in the county. The present laird has strong opinions on private ownership, and as an historian, seems to think that much too much has been made of the clearances and denies most of the recorded happenings. It was a joy to see John McGrath (of 7:84 Theatre fame) discussing these matters with "Mr" Arbuthnot in a recent television broadcast.

KINCARDINE

Land area	244,248 acres
Inland water	1,197 acres

Estates down to 5,000 acres

Owner	Estate	Acres
Sir E. W. Gladstone	Fasque	47,700
Vt. Cowdray	Dunecht	21,600
Vt. Stonehaven	Rickarton	8,100
Mrs E. S. P. Simpson	Muchalls	7,000
Unknown	Lauriston	6,500
Mrs M. C. Miller	Barras	6,200
Mrs D. Somerville	Fettercairn	5,000

Totals of Estates down to 5,000 acres

7 Estates — 102,100 acres

Estates 5,000 to 1,000 acres

Between		
5,000 and 4,000 acres:	2:	8,100 acres
4,000 and 3,000 acres:	3:	9,900 acres
3,000 and 2,000 acres:	13:	31,300 acres
2,000 and 1,000 acres:	22:	26,700 acres

Totals of Estates 5,000 to 1,000 acres

40 Estates — 76,000 acres

Summary

Estates between		
50,000 and 40,000 acres	1::	47,700 acres
30,000 and 20,000 acres:	1:	21,600 acres
10,000 and 5,000 acres:	5:	32,800 acres
5,000 and 1,000 acres:	40:	76,000 acres

Grand total of Estates down to 1,000 acres

47 Estates — 178,100 acres

Total land area of county .... 244,248 acres

Total area of private Estates down to 1,000 acres .... 178,100 acres

ANGUS

For a county of such large acreage it is interesting to find that even in 1874 there was only one estate over 100,000 acres. It was that of the Earl of Dalhousie of Brechin Castle — 136,600 acres with the very high annual value of £55,600. This estate still extends from very rich low ground to the highest parts of Angus with, however, only 43,800 acres — still the largest in Angus.

It is evident that much of the fertile land here is in the hands of comparatively small owners, without much change since 1874.

The Earl of Airlie has, however, dropped from 65,000 (£21,664) to 31,400 acres. That annual £22,000 must have been extremely useful to this noble family in those early days.

At Kinnaird Castle, the Earl of Southesk had 22,500 acres, now 12,800 acres, around 2,000 acres of which are policies, and so lost to agriculture and forestry. There appear to be ties between this family and the Duke of Fife and Royalty, through marriage.

Balnaboth in 1874 had 21,893 acres (£3,515) then owned by David Ogilvy, now by Charles Ogilvy McLean (related to the Airlies who are also Ogilvies), but now reduced to 8,400 acres.

This county is full of old nobility, including the Queen at Bachnagairn with 5,500 acres, and the Queen Mother's birthplace at Glamis where the Earl of Strathmore now owns 19,000 acres as compared with only 5,000 (£2,861) in 1874, a big step up.

But we have no Dukes in this county — I am wrong — I just remember now the Duke of Roxburghe has 18,700 acres — he had none here in 1874. This brings him well up to the 100,000 acre mark in total, as he owns huge areas in the South region.

Lord Inchcape now owns 17,300 acres, some of it acquired from Airlie estate at Tulchan.

An aristocratic, even royal, county.

ANGUS

Land area	559,090 acres
Inland water	3,353 acres

Estates down to 5,000 acres

Owner	Estate	Acres
Earl of Dalhousie	Dalhousie Ests.	43,800
Earl of Airlie	Airlie Ests.	31,400
Earl of Strathmore	Glamis Ests.	19,000
Duke of Roxburghe	Milden	18,700
W. P. R. Foster	Gannochy	17,900

51

Lord Inchcape	Tulchan-Glenogil	17,300
Sir J. Kefwick	Hunthill	16,400
Panmure Estates	Panmure	13,000
Earl of Southesk	Kinnaird Castle	12,800
Rt. Hon. G. B. Lyell	Kinnordy Ests.	11,900
Lt. Col. W. J. Campbell Adamson	Careston Ests.	11,200
Capt. C. A. O. Maclean	Balnaboth	8,400
Maj. J. P. O. Gibb	Glenisla	7,300
R. Steuart Fothringham	Fothringham	7,000
Lt. Col. H. C. Walker	Lundie Castle	6,400
Tr. of Conway Fletcher	Fearn Ests.	6,400
The Queen	Bachnagairn	5,500

Totals of Estates down to 5,000 acres

17 Estates — 254,400 acres

Estates 5,000 to 1,000 acres

Between			
	5,000 and 4,000 acres:	4:	17,600 acres
	4,000 and 3,000 acres:	11:	40,100 acres
	3,000 and 2,000 acres:	20:	49,100 acres
	2,000 and 1,000 acres:	27:	36,200 acres

Totals of Estates 5,000 to 1,000 acres

62 Estates — 143,000 acres

Summary

Estates between			
	50,000 and 40,000 acres:	1:	43,800 acres
	40,000 and 30,000 acres:	1:	31,400 acres
	20,000 and 10,000 acres:	9:	138,200 acres
	10,000 and 5,000 acres:	6:	41,000 acres
	5,000 and 1,000 acres:	62:	143,000 acres

Grand total of Estates down to 1,000 acres

80 Estates — 397,400

Total land area of county .... 559,090 acres

Total area of private Estates down to 1,000 acres .... 397,400 acres

PERTHSHIRE

This very large county I know intimately (as I do Angus). Looking over the 1874 record we are struck by the size of Breadalbane estate — 233,200 acres (£36,000) in Perthshire, continuing into Argyll with another 204,200 acres (£22,300) — a total of 437,400 acres with an

52

annual return of £60,000. This huge Campbell estate appears to have grown up during the eighteenth and nineteenth centuries and flourished until around 1900, then, fairly rapidly, disappeared completely, until the present Earl who lives in Hampstead, owns no land of any consequence. This is one of the terrible features of the landownership not only in Perthshire, but all over Scotland.

The same picture is shown by the neighbouring family of Menzies — 116,000 acres a century ago and none today. Causes of failure do not, I think, matter very much. What is fundamental is that our most precious asset can be played about with in some gambling den, or in family feuds, while the land degrades and the rural communities perish.

The one huge remaining estate, Atholl, had in 1874 194,600 acres (£36,000). It still covers 130,000 acres. Drummond Castle estate has shrunk from 76,800 acres to 65,000, Charles Home Drummond Moray at Abercairney from 40,600 acres to 13,000 acres. Another Murray (another of the very well able to look after themselves clan) has Scone Palace. In 1874 this estate was 31,197 acres with very high annual value of £23,000. This follower of Atholl has increased his holdings to 33,800 acres, all of it on high quality land. Lord Mansfield is as well known as his Chief, the Duke, but lays no claim to owning deer forests, though his father and he have been leaders in blood sports in Scotland.

The same acquisitive attitude could be credited to the Stuart Fothringhams of Grandtully and Murthly who, in 1874, owned 33,300 acres and today have reached just on 45,000 acres. About 15,000 acres of this is let to an American syndicate as a game reserve, to which sportsmen from the U.S. fly in even for a single day's shoot — one of the contemptible ways in which our Scottish landlords treat our land.

The 12,000 acre estate at Dupplin, held in 1874 by the Earl of Kinnoull, has been taken over by Lord Forteviot (Dewar's whisky). These 12,000 acres are about the most fertile in Scotland and Lord Forteviot knew what he was doing. I gather its agricultural section is well managed, but in forestry the good lord has a lot to learn.

In 1874 the Duke of Montrose had 32,300 acres — now none. The Earl of Moray, whose ancestors seem to have prowled a lot, now owns 10,800 acres, reduced from 40,600.

It is extremely difficult to trace what has happened to huge areas once owned by Campbell of Breadalbane and the Menzies. Certainly the Wills family in Glen Lyon and Rannoch now own 70,000 acres.

Meggernie estate in Glen Lyon is one of Perthshire's biggest scandals — agriculture and forestry sacrificed to game. It is sad that the game racket is responsible for the degradation of very extensive areas of our valuable grazing and forestry lands — some of which — in Perthshire — are the richest in Scotland.

There is another interesting owner in Perthshire, W. G. Gordon with 10,780 acres at Lude and another 27,000 at Arrisdale (Inverness). At one time we had a bout in *The Scotsman* about red deer. He then told me he would collect me and fly me in his plane (he is called the 'flying farmer') to show what red deer farming really meant. I never heard from him. He is another booze man, this time concerned with gin. On the 12th August he must get up at dawn to collect his packet of grouse for delivery by plane at the Government-owned posh hotel — Gleneagles — in time for lunch and dinner that day.

PERTH

Land area	1,595,804 acres
Inland water	37,036 acres

Estates down to 5,000 acres

Owner	Estates	Acres
Duke of Atholl	Atholl Estates	130,000
Earl of Ancaster	Drummond Castle	65,000
Sir Ed. Wills Bt.	Meggernie	57,900
Brig. Çolvin	Camusericht	45,000
D. Steuart Fothringham	Murthly	33,800
Earl of Mansfield	Scone	33,800
E. J. & R. N. Lowes	Glenfalloch	22,400
Capt. A. A. C. Farquharson	Invercauld	21,600
Vt. Wimbourne	Craiganour	21,200
I. C. Sales, I. Terriere	Dunalastair	20,200
R. W. Pilkington	Dalnacardoch	19,600
Ben Challon Ltd.	Glen Lochay	18,300
Mr & Mrs D. S. Bowser	Argaty & Auchline	17,700
Keir & Cawdor	Quoigs	16,400
Earl of Moray	Doune	16,300
Lord Rootes	Glen Almond	15,500
Mrs M. E. Stroyan	Boreland	15,100
Mrs Molteno	Glen Lyon	14,700
Lt. Col .I. Hornung	Dalnaspidal	13,000
Alex Spearman	Fealar	13,000
I. J. McKinlay	Auchleeks	13,000
W. S. H. Drummond-Moray	Abercairney	13,000
W. J. Denby-Roberts	Strathallan	12,500
Marquis of Lansdowne	Meikleour	12,400
Lord Forteviot	Dupplin	12,100
A. R. Ward	Kinnaird	12,000
J. D. Hutchison	Bolfracks	11,800

Wills Family	Innerwick	11,800
Sir J. H. I. Whitaker	Auchnafree	11,800
Mr MacNaughton	Inverlochlarig	11,700
H. Steuart Fothringham	Grandtully	11,500
W. G. Gordon	Lude	10,700
J. F. Priestly	Innergeldie	10,700
Sir J. Amory	Glenfernate	10,200
Mr Curzon	Dunan	10,200
J. Cameron	Glen Finglass	10,000
Glen Devon Ests. Ltd.	Glen Devon	9,800
Sir W. F. K. Murray	Ochertyre	9,300
Maj. N. C. Ramsay	Farleyer	8,900
Mrs M. Constable	Glasclune	8,900
Sir M. G. Nairne	Pitcarmick	8,300
Mrs M. B. Hatford	Moness	8,000
W. Taylor	Ardeonaig	7,900
Maj. D. H. Butter	Cluniemore	7,300
J. D. Miller	Remony	7,300
W. J. Christie	Loch Dochart	7,200
Lord Dundee	Kinnell	7,200
Lord Cadogan	Snaigow, Glen Quaich	7,200
Unknown	Stronvar	6,900
D. Winton	Dalmunzie	6,600
W. J. Webber	Kynachan	6,200
The Master of Kinnaird	Rossie Priory	5,800
More Farm Prop. Ltd.	Ardtalnaig	5,700
Stewart Duff	Strelitz	5,700
Dr Watters	Edinample	5,700
Hon. R. J. Eden	Cromlix	5,700
Mrs Joynson	Ledard	5,400
Sir R. Orr-Ewing Bt.	Cardross	5,300
Sir Stanley Norie-Millar	Murrayshall	5,100
P. Rattray of Rattray	Rattray Castle	5,000
Gleneagles Est. Tr.	Gleneagles	5,000
Wild Life Trust	Coire Bhachaidh	5,000

Totals of Estates down to 5,000 acres

62 Estates — 972,300 acres

Estates 5,000 to 1,000 acres

Between			
	5,000 and 4,000 acres:	18:	82,400 acres
	4,000 and 3,000 acres:	33:	107,300 acres
	3,000 and 2,000 acres:	49:	119,700 acres
	2,000 and 1,000 acres:	86:	114,400 acres

Totals of Estates 5,000 to 1,000 acres

186 Estates — 423,800

Summary

Estates between			
	100,000 acres upwards:	1:	130,000 acres
	75,000 and 50,000 acres:	2;	122,900 acres
	50,000 and 40,000 acres:	1:	45,000 acres
	40,000 and 30,000 acres:	2:	67,600 acres
	30,000 and 20,000 acres:	4:	85,400 acres
	20,000 and 10,000 acres:	26:	345,000 acres
	10,000 and 5,000 acres:	26:	176,400 acres
	5,000 and 1,000 acres:	186:	423,800 acres

Grand total of Estates down to 1,000 acres

248 Estates — 1,396,100 acres

Total land area of County ....1,595,804 acres

Total area of private Estates down to 1,000 acres ....1,396,100 acres

Summary of Estates down to 1,000 acres in the North East plus Perthshire

In Thousands

COUNTY	100 +		100/75		75/50		50/40		40/30		30/20		20/10		10/5		5/1	
	Est.	Acres	Est.	Acres	Est.	Acres	Est.	Acres	Est.	Acres	Est.	Acres	Est.	Acres	Est.	Acres	Est.	Acres
NAIRN	—	—	—	—	—	—	—	—	1	38.3	—	—	1	15.9	1	5.5	8	17.1
MORAY	—	—	—	—	1	57.5	—	—	—	—	1	23.9	4	51.5	4	27.5	20	43.5
BANFF	—	—	—	—	—	—	1	41.4	1	33.9	—	—	4	47.2	4	31.9	29	72.9
ABERDEEN	—	—	1	75.0	2	116.8	—	—	—	—	6	150.4	12	149.4	23	147.7	110	287.3
KINCARDINE	—	—	—	—	—	—	1	47.7	—	—	1	21.6	—	—	5	32.8	40	76.0
ANGUS	—	—	—	—	—	—	1	43.8	1	31.4	—	—	9	138.2	6	41.0	62	143.0
PERTHSHIRE	1	130.0	—	—	2	122.9	1	45.0	2	67.6	4	85.4	27	363.4	26	176.4	186	423.8
TOTALS	1	130.0	1	75.0	5	297.2	4	177.6	5	171.2	12	281.3	57	765.6	69	462.8	455	1063.6

SOUTH REGION (S)

This region has 18 counties from Clackmannan to the Borders.

There are 594 private estates down to 1,000 acres with 2,452,600 acres.

    With regard to this region I think I should state here that it is unlike the other two in that a very small amount of the West and NE has been left unsurveyed by Millman, but in the South there are quite extensive areas untouched, as is evidenced by the relatively small area recorded in some counties against the total for the county. Another distinguishing feature of the South is that several counties display a significant shortage of private estates compared to the other two regions.

Clackmannan
Kinross
Fife
Dumbarton
Stirling
W. Lothian
Midlothian
E. Lothian
Renfrew
Lanark
Peebles
Selkirk
Berwick
Ayr
Wigtown
Dumfries
Kirkcudbright
Roxburgh

The South

CLACKMANNAN

This is the smallest county in Scotland, but, being in the central belt, one of those which set the pace in the industrialisation of Scotland.

Straight away, in the 1874 survey, we find those grasping Scone Palace chaps owning 1,705 acres worth £1,751 p.a. plus £1,886.9 annually from coal. The Earl of Zetland was also in this profitable venture, owning 2,726 acres worth £3,276 p.a. and coal £2,635. Worth how much in today's figures?

Another four noted landlords who were claiming a rake off from coal were Lord Burleigh, the Earl of Kellie, Sir Andrew Orr and Robert Balfour Wardlaw Ramsay of Tillicoultry, together claiming £16,629 in rents and £3,300 in coal levies.

The above six noble Scottish families must have been among the first to get rich on the blood, sweat and tears of men, women and children slaving in the mines.

There was only one large estate in 1874. Lord Abercromby's, Airthry Castle had 3,700 acres (£5,200), today adjoining and part of Stirling University. The picture is not dissimilar today, only one estate reaching the 5,000 acre mark, but the land here is so very fertile that 'One link of Forth is worth an Earldom in the North'.

CLACKMANNAN

Land area	34,860 acres
Inland water	290 acres

Estates down to 5,000 acres

Owner	Estates	Acres
J. Miller	Rhodders	5,000

Totals of Estates down to 5,000 acres

1 Estate — 5,000 acres

60

Estates 5,000 to 1,000 acres

Between			
4,000 and 3,000 acres:	1:	3,000 acres
3,000 and 2,000 acres:	4:	9,600 acres
2,000 and 1,000 acres:	7:	9,200 acres

Totals of Estates 5,000 to 1,000 acres

12 Estates — 21,800 acres

Summary

Estates between			
10,000 and 5,000 acres:	1:	5,000 acres
5,000 and 1,000 acres;	12:	21,800 acres

Grand total of Estates down to 1,000 acres

13 Estates — 26,800 acres

Total land area of county .... 34,860 acres

Total land area of private Estates down to 1,000 acres .... 26,800 acres

KINROSS

This is a much quieter county than Clackmannan, with no estate of 5,000 acres and no serious industrial aspect. A good deal of the land is marginal. I repeat, it is a quiet-going countryside of few changes, unlike any other county in Scotland — desirable? Ledlanet of 'Ledlanet Nights' fame is within this county and owned by the publisher John Calder.

KINROSS

Land area	52,392 acres
Inland water	3,457 acres

Estates down to 5,000 acres

NIL

Estates 5,000 to 1,000 acres

Between			
4,000 and 3,000 acres:	2:	6,800 acres
3,000 and 2,000 acres:	1:	2,200 acres
2,000 and 1,000 acres:	6:	9,400 acres

Totals of Estates 5,000 to 1,000 acres

9 Estates — 18,400 acres

Summary

Estates between   5,000 and 1,000 acres;   9:   18,400 acres

Grand total of Estates down to 1,000 acres

9 Estates — 18,400 acres

Total land area of county .... 52,392 acres

Total land area of private Estates down to 1,000 acres .... 18,400 acres

FIFE

This is amongst the most disturbed counties in Scotland with its coal and varied industries, but I stress coal. Its bings are still a scandal and disgrace and quite unfit for human beings to live near. Ten years ago Fife County Council under its able forward-looking amenity officer Maurice Taylor, an Englishman, began to reclaim four square miles of this butchered land, at a cost (then) of just over £7,000 per acre. This work proved to be highly successful, but with public money of course!

Estates, again, are smaller in this county. There were two in 1874 over the 10,000 acre mark, Balbirnie owned by a Balfour (same family as A.J.B.) of 10,600 acres (£14,500 plus coal £530) and Lathrisk 10,000 acres — no coal. The Balfours remain there today with around 7,000 acres, one of the largest owners in Fife and, as already noted, owning a big chunk of Sutherland.

The largest owners today are the Wemyss family, with 8,800 acres almost the same as they held in 1874 (£15,200 — coal £8,600). This family turns up everywhere in the South. In 1874 the Gilmours of Lundin owned only 2,728 acres, but today the MP Sir John Gilmour has 6,800 acres of fertile land in this county, plus, it seems, much more in these southern areas under the names 'Lundin, Montrave and Dalmahoy'.

The Earl of Moray owned in 1874 7,500 acres (£8,700 — coal £2,800). Today he still owns 5,400 acres. The Munro-Fergusons of Raith had 7,135 acres (£12,337 — coal £1,582). They still have 5,000 acres here but also the huge estate of Novar in Ross. Twenty years ago, a close friend of mine, Frank Scott, in his day Scotland's leading forester, was asked by the owner of Raith to mark, measure, value, licence and sell a large quantity of very valuable old timber in his policies. Scott asked me to help, and after very intensive hard work,

£91,000 was got for the timber. Around £20,000 was paid at once by the merchant. Scott's bill for the work done was around £1,700, but Mr Luttrell (he had not yet changed his name to Munro-Ferguson) would only pay instalments over an extended period, to which we took exception. It went to arbitration, we lost and as losers had to pay the full bill: £80! Landlords!! Once more showing their inherently arrogant, mean streak.

The Earl of Zetland appears, far from home. In 1874 he held 5,600 acres (£8,339 — coal £832) but his family name was Dundas, so he was probably related to Dundas of Arniston, Midlothian. Zetland is not noted in Fife at the present time. At that time he owned 13,600 acres in Shetland and 30,000 in Orkney.

Sir R. Anstruther of Balcaskie is another of those wanderers in search of land. He owned in 1874 35,600 acres in Caithness and in Fife 2,121 acres (£5,062 — coal £53). Today his successors own 15,300 acres in Caithness and a small area in Fife. A fourth estate should be mentioned. Falkland in 1874 had 7,000 acres (£10,000) owned by a Bruce. Today it remains about 6,000 acres, stated to be owned by Falkland Estates Trustees, but this probably means the Crichton Stewarts — the Bute family.

FIFE

Land area	322,856 acres
Inland water	2,289 acres

Estates down to 5,000 acres

Owner	Estates	Acres
Earl of Wemyss & March	Wemyss Ests.	8,800
Mr & Mrs J. C. Balfour	Balbirnie Ests.	6,900
Sir J. Gilmour M.P.	Montrave Estates Dalmahoy Ests.	6,800
Falkland Estate Tr.	Falkland Ests.	5,500
Earl of Moray	Moray Ests.	5,400
A. B. L. Munro-Ferguson of Novar	Raith Ests.	5,000
Unknown	Flisk	5,000
Earl of Crawford & others	Melville Ests.	5,000

Totals of Estates down to 5,000 acres

8 Estates — 48,400 acres

Estates of 5,000 to 1,000 acres

Between		
4,000 and 3,000 acres: 2:	6,500 acres
3,000 and 2,000 acres: 13:	30,800 acres
2,000 and 1,000 acres: 18:	25,600 acres

Totals of Estates 5,000 to 1,000 acres

33 Estates — 62,900 acres

Summary

| Estates between | 10,000 and 5,000 acres: 8: | 48,400 acres |
| | 5,000 and 1,000 acres: 33: | 62,900 acres |

Grand total of Estates down to 1,000 acres

41 Estates — 111,300 acres

Total land area of county .... 322,856 acres

Total area of private Estates down to 1,000 acres .... 111,300 acres

DUMBARTON

In 1874 about 50 per cent of this county was owned by the Colquhoun family of Luss — 67,000 acres (£12,848 annually). They remain there in 1970 with 42,700 acres in spite of the growth of industry. Today it is the only very big estate, but a century ago there was another of 6,800 acres owned by the Duke of Argyll.

There are more medium-sized estates here now than there were 100 years ago — 29 in place of 20.

It is our only county which is divided into two parts — both Stirling and Lanark managing to intervene.

DUMBARTON

| Land area | 154,462 acres |
| Inland water | 13,531 acres |

Estates down to 5,000 acres

Owner	Estates	Acres
Sir I. I. Colquhoun	Luss Ests.	42,700

Totals of Estates down to 5,000 acres

1 Estate — 42,700 acres

Estates 5,000 to 1,000 acres

Between	5,000 and 4,000 acres: 1:	4,500 acres
	4,000 and 3,000 acres: 4:	13,900 acres
	3,000 and 2,000 acres: 10:	25,200 acres
	2,000 and 1,000 acres: 12:	17,000 acres

Totals of Estates 5,000 to 1,000 acres

29 Estates — 60,600 acres

Summary

Estates between	50,000 and 40,000 acres: 1:	42,700 acres
	5,000 and 1,000 acres: 29:	60,600 acres

Grand totals of Estates down to 1,000 acres

30 Estates — 103,300 acres acres

Total land area of county .... 154,462 acres

Total area of private Estates down to 1,000 acres .... 103,300 acres

STIRLING

Like Dumbarton, Stirling had only one huge estate, the Duke of Montrose's at 69,000 acres (£15,700) in 1874, now reduced to a mere 8,800 acres, and the Duke, a complete absentee, in Rhodesia supporting Smith.

But there were several other large owners — e.g. Callander House — 13,000 acres owned by Forbes — now 6,600 acres; Duntreath Castle, then 9,778 acres, now 10,200 acres. Duntreath had a very high income from 'minerals' — coal? £8,500 p.a.

The old record shows a good many smaller estates, but I only record that owned by our friend the Marquis of Zetland, again at Kerse House, with 4,700 acres (£9,600 and a rich coal addition of £4,300). This laird certainly knew what he was doing.

STIRLING

Land area	288,345 acres
Inland water	8,786 acres

Estates down to 5,000 acres

Owner	Estates	Acres
Sir A. Edmonston	Duntreath Castle	10,200
Duke of Montrose	Montrose Ests.	8,800
Sir Ian F. C. Bolton Bt.	Sauchieburn	6,900
Herbertshire Tr.		
Gavin S. Davie	Callander Ests.	6,600
Unknown	Ballincleroch	6,300

Totals of Estates down to 5,000 acres

5 Estates — 38,800 acres

Estates of 5,000 to 1,000 acres

Between
4,000 and 1,000 acres:	6:	20,900 acres
3,000 and 2,000 acres:	17:	38,000 acres
2,000 and 1,000 acres:	32:	46,000 acres

Totals of Estates 5,000 to 1,000 acres

55 Estates — 104,900 acres

Summary

Estates between
20,000 and 10,000 acres:	1:	10,200 acres
10,000 and 5,000 acres:	4:	28,600 acres
5,000 and 1,000 acres:	55	104,900 acres

Grand total of Estates down to 1,000 acres

60 Estates — 143,700 acres

Total land area of county .... 288,345 acres

Total area of private Estates down to 1,000 acres .... 143,700 acres

WEST LOTHIAN

This small central county with considerable mine workings had, in 1874, the Hopetoun estate with 11,870 acres (£19,000, minerals £1,600).

Roseberry had 5,680 acres (£8,900 — coal £2,400) and the Polkennet estate had 4,300 acres (£2,800 — coal £3,600).

The remaining estates, though smaller, had often very high annual returns in minerals e.g. Torbanehill, Bathgate, with only 709 acres (£800) made £13,100 annually from minerals. Similarly, the Duke of Hamilton with 3,700 acres 'earned' £8,100 annually from minerals, besides land rents.

WEST LOTHIAN

Land area	76,855 acres
Inland water	549 acres

Estates down to 5,000 acres

NIL

Estates of 5,000 to 1,000 acres

Between
5,000 and 4,000 acres:	1:	4,400 acres
4,000 and 3,000 acres:	3:	11,000 acres
3,000 and 2,000 acres:	3:	8,500 acres
2,000 and 1,000 acres:	10:	14,000 acres

Totals of Estates 5,000 to 1,000 acres

17 Estates — 37,900 acres

Summary

Estates of 5,000 to 1,000 acres: 17:   37,900 acres

Grand total of Estates down to 1,000 acres

17 Estates — 37,0000 acres

Total land area of county .... 76,855 acres

Total area of private Estates down to 1,000 .... 37,900 acres

MIDLOTHIAN

In 1874 the Roseberry estates covered 15,600 acres of the county (£9,000 — coal £200). Now they are 12,500 acres.

Robert Dundas of Arniston had 10,200 acres (£9,500 and the coal £4,300). The estate is now 10,400 acres. I am interested to know that Dundas is the family name of the Earl of Zetland who crops up repeatedly.

Sir G. D. Clerk of Penicuik had 12,700 acres (£9,000 — coal £2,400). This estate is now 7,300 acres.

Dalmahoy, 9,000 acres (£9,000) was owned by the Earl of Morton. Now at 7,200 acres it is owned by 'Sir John Gilmour and others'.

Stair estates covered 9,700 acres here as well as huge areas in Wigtown. Buccleuch had 3,500 acres (£16,200 — coal £1,500 and £10,600 for Leith harbour — grossing £28,300 yearly from this small county alone in 1874).

Wemyss came in a small way with 1,504 acres and the Marquis of Lothian with 4,547 acres — both extremely profitable holdings.

Buccleuch now holds 2,600 acres here and Lothian 2,300 acres.

This wading through the old records and the follow-up in '70 is fascinating to me but time-consuming.

In 1874 there were a further 39 estates benefiting financially from an annual coal revenue in Midlothian. Perhaps part of the fascination I have mentioned is occasioned by my having come in touch, personally, with so many of our noble owners — in their woodlands, not, thank goodness, their mining 'activities'.

Land area	234,389 acres
Inland water	2,267 acres

Estates down to 5,000 acres

Owner	*Estates*	*Acres*
Lord Roseberry	Roseberry Ests.	12,500
Tr. late Lord Whitburgh	Borthwick Ests.	10,000
Tr. late Col. Sir R. Dundas	Dundas Ests.	10,400
Sir J. D. Clerk's 1966 Tr.	Penicuik	7,300
Sir J. Gilmour & others	Dalmahoy Ests.	7,200
Boundary clearly defined		6,200
but no facts		5,800

Totals of Estates down to 5,000 acres

7 Estates — 59,400 acres

Estates of 5,000 to 1,000 acres

Between		
5,000 and 4,000 acres:	2:	8,500 acres
4,000 and 3,000 acres:	2:	7,400 acres
3,000 and 2,000 acres:	10:	24,300 acres
2,000 and 1,000 acres:	13:	16,100 acres

Totals of Estates 5,000 to 1,000 acres

27 Estates — 56,300 acres

Summary

Estates between		
20,000 and 10,000 acres:	3:	32,900 acres
10,000 and 5,000 acres:	4:	26,500 acres
5,000 and 1,000 acres:	27:	56,300 acres

Grand total of Estates down to 1,000 acres

34 Estates — 115,700 acres

Total land area of county .... 234,389 acres

Total are of private Estates down to 1,000 acres .... 115,700 acres

EAST LOTHIAN

After measuring the estates on Millman's maps for this county, I became baffled by names which would not correspond with those on his Index sheets. After spending hours on this, I went to the Public Library where *Who's Who* showed me that Lord Binning and Lord Haddington are the same family, son and father. This was by no means the only time I had to go to *Who's Who*.

In 1874, Lord Haddington owned 8,302 acres (£13,700) at Tynninghame. This estate, now 13,000 acres, is presently owned by Lord Binning.

The biggest estate in 1874 was Tweeddale with 20,500 acres. Now this is reduced to 1,600 acres. Perhaps it is not surprising that the present Marquis of Tweeddale, now lobster farming on the west coast, remarks in *Who's Who* that he is now "striving to exist after Dynamic Socialism". But who, or what, was responsible for the downfall of the Tweeddale estate with an annual intake of £11,500? Can the Marquis enlighten us?

Then, in 1874 we had Whittinghame — 10,600 acres (£10,600) owned by A. J. Balfour, one of our Tory prime ministers, but not appearing among the estates today of 5,000 acres upwards.

Wemyss appears again, probably because of the coal, with 10,000 acres (£22,300 — coal £226). We shall hear much more of the Earl of Wemyss and March as a landlord.

The Duke of Roxburghe today owns 8,400 acres in East Lothian, while in 1874 he had only 3,900 here.

Only 13 estates in this county were connected with mines.

EAST LOTHIAN

Land area	171,044 acres
Inland water	421 acres

Estates down to 5,000 acres

Owner	Estates	Acres
Tr. of Lord Binning	Tyninghame	13,000
Duke of Roxburghe	Roxburgh Ests.	8,400
Earl of Wemyss & March	Wemyss Ests.	7,000
Duke of Hamilton	Hamilton Ests.	5,200

Totals of Estates down to 5,000 acres

4 Estates — 33,600 acres

Estates of 5,000 to 1,000 acres

Between		
4,000 and 3,000 acres:	3:	10,500 acres
3,000 and 2,000 acres:	2	5,200 acres
2,000 and 1,000 acres:	21:	26,500 acres

Totals of Estates 5,000 to 1,000 acres

26 Estates — 42,200 acres

69

Summary

Estates between   20,000 and 10,000 acres: 1:   13,000 acres
                    10,000 and 5,000 acres: 3:   20,600 acres
                     5,000 and 1,000 acres: 26:   42,200 acres

Grand total of Estates down to 1,000 acres

30 Estates — 75,800 acres

Total land area of county .... 171,044 acres

Total area of private Estates down to 1,000 acres .... 75,800 acres

RENFREW

It always seem strange to me that every county (except the very small ones) has its massive estate(s) — in this one, Ardgowan, in 1874 had 25,000 acres owned by Sir M. R. Shaw Stewart. Even today, reduced to 10,800 acres, it is a big chunk of land.

The now famous 1895 'Red Deer Commission' had a Shaw Stewart of Ardgowan as a member. He seemed a quiet sort of chap, and along with the others, must have done a pile of work.

Eaglesham was the only other large estate here in 1874, with 16,500 acres with annual return of £12,000, a tidy sum. In total there were 18 estates which profited £20,000 each year from coal. Quarrying also was profitable for the landlord, 20 or so estates sharing £7,000 p.a.

This is the only county which records the unusual asset of timber ponds. There were 11 of them on the Clyde and they remain vividly in my mind when I recall sailing down past them in the 'Lord of the Isles' or the old 'Minard Castle'. These 'ponds' were sections of the south bank of the river fenced off, in which stocks of imported timber, belonging to local timber merchants, were stored until required for breaking-down in their sawmills.

This is one of the counties with quite large areas without boundaries of estates marked by Millman. Thus I can account for only 60,000 acres out of 144,000.

There were two interesting small estates in 1874. The Homes of the Hirsel held 1,325 acres (£3,100 — coal £400), Sir Wm. Maxwell of Pollok and Keir owned 4,800 acres (£13,000 — coal £500). Quite useful additions to income at that time.

70

RENFREW

Land area		143,829 acres
Inland water		2,941 acres

Estates down to 5,000 acres

Owner	Estates	Acres
Sir W. G. Shaw-Stewart	Ardgowan	10,800
R. Munro	Polnoon	7,000
Unknown	Neilstonside	5,000

Totals of Estates down to 5,000 acres

3 Estates — 22,800 acres

Estates of 5,000 to 1,000 acres

Between			
	5,000 and 4,000 acres:	1:	4,100 acres
	4,000 and 3,000 acres:	1:	3,300 acres
	3,000 and 2,000 acres:	5:	14,600 acres
	2,000 and 1,000 acres:	10:	14,300 acres

Totals of Estates 5,000 to 1,000 acres

17 Estates — 36,300 acres

Summary

Estates between			
	20,000 and 10,000 acres:	1:	10,800 acres
	10,000 and 5,000 acres:	2:	12,000 acres
	5,000 and 1,000 acres:	17;	36,300 acres

Grand total of Estates down to 1,000 acres

20 Estates — 59,100 acres

Total land area of county .... 143,829 acres

Total area of private Estates down to 1,000 acres .... 59,100 acres

LANARK

It is not surprising that Lanark is considered to be the county that has suffered most through industrialisation, when we read in the 1874 records that 199 estates were then making big incomes from coal mining. I did not invent this figure. Thousands of acres were being exploited, and the mining companies, closely linked with such owners as our Buccleuchs, Wemysses, Hamiltons, Butes, etc., were allowed to leave the countryside in the usual unholy mess.

At that time we had five huge estates here. The Home family held 61,900 acres (£24,800 — coal £4,700). This estate in Lanark is still 48,000 acres.

The Duke of Hamilton held 45,700 acres which he must have driven to the limit to get £38,400 plus £56,920 for coal. He must now own much less in this county, as I have not unearthed him from the maps.

The old Lee and Carnwath estate, (now Dunsyre and owned by S. F. MacDonald Lockhart) was 31,600 acres, but, as far as I can ascertain, is now down to 20,000 acres; but subject to correction.

Two further estates then making handsome incomes from coal, Abington House 30,000 acres (£10,000 — coal £100) and Lord Hopetoun's unnamed estate 20,000 acres (£3,200 — coal £2,300) have now disappeared.

The Duke of Buccleuch had his share (10,000 acres) here also, as had others. Today the big boys are Lord Linlithgow, Lords Sorn and Rotherwick, one of those Private Forestry Groups (7,200 acres) and finally Buccleuch again.

Lanark is a sad county in many ways.

LANARK

Land area	574,473 acres
Inland water	4,750 acres

Estates down to 5,000 acres

Owner	Estates	Acres
Sir Alec Douglas Home	Douglas & Angus Ests.	48,000
Lord Linlithgow	Linlithgow Ests.	23,000
S. F. MacDonald-Lockhart	Dunsyre	20,000
Lords Sorn & Rotherwick	Lanfine Ests.	11,000
Private Forestry Group	Private Forestry	7,200
Duke of Buccleuch	Buccleuch Ests.	5,500

Totals of Estates down to 5,000 acres

6 Estates — 114,700 acres

Estates of 5,000 to 1,000 acres

Between			
	5,000 and 4,000 acres:	3:	12,000 acres
	4,000 and 3,000 acres:	3:	10,100 acres
	3,000 and 2,000 acres:	6:	14,100 acres
	2,000 and 1,000 acres:	16:	21,800 acres

Totals of Estates 5,000 to 1,000 acres

28 Estates — 58,000 acres

72

Summary

Estates between				
	50,000 and 40,000 acres:	1:	48,000 acres
	30,000 and 20,000 acres:	2:	43,000 acres
	20,000 and 10,000 acres:	1:	11,000 acres
	10,000 and 5,000 acres:	2:	12,700 acres
	5,000 and 1,000 acres:	28:	58,000 acres

Grand total of Estates down to 1,000 acres

34 Estates — 172,700 acres

Total land area of county .... 574,473 acres

Total area of private Estates down to 1,000 acres .... 172,700 acres

PEEBLES

This is a small, quiet county. In 1874 the only very big estate belonged to Wemyss — 41,200 acres. This is now reduced to 16,000 acres, unusual in the case of this family.

The noted estate of Traquair had 10,800 acres but only holds 6,000 now.

There is no mention of Roseberry estates in 1874, but they now claim 12,000 acres.

I shall not go on any further regarding this quiet-going county.

PEEBLES

Land area		222,240 acres
Inland water		1,048 acres

Estates down to 5,000 acres

Owner	Estates	Acres
Countess of Dysart	Stobo	16,200
Lord Roseberry	Roseberry Ests.	12,000
J. T. S. Morton-Robertson	Portmore	8,200
Lt. Col. A. M. Sprot	Haystoun	6,800
W. Reid	Glencatho	6,200
P. D. Maxwell-Stewart	Traquair	5,900
Tr. Mrs E. Marshall	Baddinsgall	5,500
Messrs. Dykes	S. Slipperfield	5,500
Col. D. G. C. Sutherland	N. Slipperfield	5,000

Totals of Estates down to 5,000 acres

9 Estates — 71,300 acres

Estates of 5,000 to 1,000 acres

Between			
5,000 and 4,000 acres:	2:	8,900 acres
4,000 and 3,000 acres:	2:	7,400 acres
3,000 and 2,000 acres:	5:	13,500 acres
2,000 and 1,000 acres:	9:	11,700 acres

Totals of Estates down to 1,000 acres

18 Estates — 41,500 acres

Summary

Estates between			
20,000 and 10,000 acres:	2:	28,200 acres
10,000 and 5,000 acres:	7:	43,100 acres
5,000 and 1,000 acres:	18:	41,500 acres

Grand total of Estates down to 1,000 acres

27 Estates — 112,800 acres

Total land area of County .... 222,240 acres

Total area of private Estates down to 1,000 acres .... 112,800 acres

SELKIRK

Another small, quiet county, the most notable feature of which is, perhaps, the Duke of Buccleuch. His estate was 60,400 acres in 1874 and is now, surprisingly, 30,000. On the other hand, we find no Wemyss land here in the old record, but now they have 21,000 acres. Did Buccleuch and Wemyss make some sort of exchange? This is the mad kind of treatment to which our land is often subjected, all over Scotland. No continuity of management.

Apart from these two owners, the only large present-day one is one of the private 'Forestry Groups'.

There is no trace on today's maps of the noted Traquair and Thirlestane estates which used to belong to Lord Napier. The Duke of Sutherland, interestingly, now owns 1,000 acres here — even Dukes find landowning tricky. Not so long ago Sutherland's Duke held a million acres in the North — now none. Could this sort of thing possibly happen to Buccleuch?

Philliphaugh estate is also interesting. In 1874 it had 1,857 acres, and was owned by Sir J. Murray of Philliphaugh and Melgund. In his inventory sheets, Millman mentions this estate three times, and, as in other cases, I had considerable difficulty in locating the pieces of land claimed by this estate on the 1" maps. I found the estate now totals 7,000 acres, owned by the wealthy industrialist Sir Wm . Strang-Steel. There must be many other fragmented estates that I have not been able to piece together as I did this one, as it is extremely time-consuming.

SELKIRK

Land area	171,209 acres
Inland water	1,797 acres

Estates down to 5,000 acres

Owner	Estates	Acres
Duke of Buccleuch	Buccleuch Ests.	29,600
Earl of Wemyss & March	Wemyss Ests.	20,900
Private Forestry Group	Private Forestry	6,500

Totals of Estates down to 5,000 acres

3 Estates — 57,000 acres

Estates of 5,000 to 1,000 acres

Between			
	4,000 and 3,000 acres:	1:	3,200 acres
	3,000 and 2,000 acres:	9:	19,900 acres
	2,000 and 1,000 acres:	11:	17,800 acres

Totals of Estates 5,000 to 1,000 acres

21 Estates — 40,900 acres

Summary

Estates between			
	30,000 and 20,000 acres:	2:	50,500 acres
	10,000 and 5,000 acres:	1:	6,500 acres
	5,000 and 1,000 acres:	21:	40,900 acres

Grand total of Estates down to 1,000 acres

25 Estates — 97,900 acres

Total land area of County .... 171,209 acres

Total area of private Estates down to 1,000 acres .... 97,900 acres

BERWICK

One of the counties bordering England — on which border 'feudal superiority' ends. But that is another story.

In 1874, Thirlestane Castle and the Lauder Estate belonged to

F

Lord Lauderdale with 24,700 acres (now 18,100 acres) and Marchmont belonged to Lord Campbell with 20,200 acres — now reduced to 5,000 and owned by Sir John McEwen (no relation!).

The Earl of Haddington then had 14,300 acres, now 9,200. The Hirsel of Douglas Home fame was 10,300 acres, now 5,500. The Marquis of Tweeddale used to hold 18,100 acres here — now gone.

The present laird, we remember, is looking for lobsters on the west coast, but still manages to hold good company with the Pearsons (Cowdray), the Atholls and the Nobles.

The Duke of Roxburghe's lands appear to have been reduced in acreage here too.

The Duke of Sutherland holds some land here. I have not been able to trace what has become of much of the land lost to the above estates perhaps because of large blank spaces in the copies of maps put at my disposal.

BERWICK

Land area	292,535 acres
Inland water	1,359 acres

Estates down to 5,000 acres

Owner	Estates	Acres
Duke of Roxburghe	Roxburgh Ests.	12,900
Frank J. Usher	Dunglas	9,700
Billie Castle Estates	Billie Castle	9,500
Earl of Haddington	Tyninghame (Mellerstain) Est.	9,200
Countess of Lauderdale	Lauder Ests.	8,100
A. F. Fisher	Brockholes	6,900
Mr Calder	Billie Mains	6,500
J. L. McDougal	Blythe	5,900
Sir Alec Douglas Home	The Hirsel	5,500
Ladykirk Estates Ltd.	Ladykirk	5,500
Sir John McEwen	Marchmont	5,000
Duke of Sutherland	Mertoun House	5,000

Totals of Estates down to 5,000 acres

12 Estates — 89,700 acres

Estates of 5,000 to 1,000 acres

Between			
	5,000 and 4,000 acres:	2:	8,100 acres
	4,000 and 3,000 acres:	5:	18,800 acres
	3,000 and 2,000 acres:	10:	22,700 acres
	2,000 and 1,000 acres:	17:	21,000 acres

Totals of Estates 5,000 to 1,000 acres

34 Estates — 70,600 acres

Summary

Estates between	20,000 and 10,000 acres:	1:	12,900 acres
	10,000 and 5,000 acres:	11:	76,800 acres
	5,000 and 1,000 acres:	34:	70,600 acres

Grand total of Estates down to 1,000 acres

46 Estates — 160,300 acres

Total land area of county .... 292,535 acres

Total area of private Estates down to 1,000 acres .... 160,300 acres

AYR

There are many regrettable blanks in the maps of this large county, from which I must deduce today's owners. In 1874 there were 110 estates drawing income from coal. The Marquess of Ailsa had 76,000 acres, now down to 21,100 acres. The Marquess of Bute had 44,000 acres, bringing in £22,800 for land and £2,500 for coal each year. The Butes were noted coal-hunters. So far as I can ascertain they hold no land here now.

Twenty thousand acres at Cambusdoon were owned by the Baird Coal Company (£8,000 — coal £1,000). This estate too has evaporated.

Mrs Jean Macadam Cathcart owned Berbeth, Dalmellington worth £9,427 plus £8,734 annually for coal — great wealth wrung from the bitter labour of workers, men, women and children.

The Earl of Eglinton with 23,600 acres creamed off £46,600 in rents, £10,000 from coal and Eglinton had an added bonus of £4,500 p.a. thrown in for harbour, a total of £61,000 every year.

From South of the border, we had our friend who also appeared in Caithness, the Duke of Portland, with 25,000 acres earning him an annual £60,500, from land, coal, harbour. Not listed in 1970.

Fergusson of Kilkerran who had 22,630 acres in 1874 worth £13,500 p.a. is one of these 1874 owners who appears in the '70 maps, with 9,500 acres.

There were nine smaller estates netting £80,000 from land and coal each year. Of these, Lanfine appears today to have grown from 10,000 acres to 12,000. They are all noted in the lists in this book.

I am sorry about the omissions there must be in this county, and these should, I hope will, be rectified, but I keep repeating: an official Government register is the only answer.

When I was dealing with this county I was puzzled in not having the name of owners and now I am grateful to my friend Willie Ross M.P. for Kilmarnock for his query in Hansard and the reply which supplies the name.

Oral Question (Hansard 23rd May 1977):

Mr William Ross: "Is my hon. friend aware that among farmers in the Kilmarnock area there is much more concern about the savage increases in rents by the local landowner, Kilmarnock Estates, owned by Lord Howard de Walden, than there is about the C.A.P. prices? There is a limit to what we can do about the C.A.P. prices, but surely we can do something about these rent increases at home".

There is no mention of Kilmarnock Estates in 1874.

AYR

Land area	724,234 acres
Inland water	6,594 acres

Estates down to 5,000 acres

Owner	Estates	Acres
Marquis of Ailsa	Cassillis	21,100
Lord Inchcape	Glenapp	19,600
Lords Sorn & Rotherwick	Lanfine Ests.	12,000
Lord Howard de Walden	Kilmarnock Ests.	11,500
Charles Fergusson	Kilkerran Ests.	9,500
Lady Jean Campbell	Loudoun	8,800
Knock Castle Estates	Knock Castle	8,800
Sir G. Hughes-Onslow	Alton Albany	8,200
Lord Houldsworth	Kirkbride Ests.	7,500
R. G. Angus	Ladykirk	7,200
R. S. Beale	Drumlan Ford	7,100
Marchioness Douro	Kinockdolian	6,000

Totals of Estates down to 5,000 acres

12 Estates — 127,300 acres

Estates of 5,000 to 1,000 acres

Between		
4,000 and 3,000 acres: 5:	17,800 acres
3,000 and 2,000 acres: 11:	23,000 acres
2,000 and 1,000 acres: 15:	21,000 acres

78

Totals of Estates 5,000 to 1,000 acres

31 Estates — 61,800 acres

Summary

Estates between			
	20,000 and 10,000 acres:	4:	64,200 acres
	10,000 and 5,000 acres:	8:	63,100 acres
	5,000 and 1,000 acres:	31:	61,800 acres

Grand total of Estates down to 1,000 acres

43 Estates — 189,100 acres

Total land area of county .... 724,234 acres

Total land area of private Estates down to 1,000 acres .... 189,100 acres

WIGTOWN

This smallish county is dominated by the massive estate of Stair with 105,000 acres showing on Millman's maps (but some of it marked 'about to be sold').

In 1874 Stair's holding was 79,200 acres worth £40,400 p.a. At that time Bute had 20,200 acres, but much of this seems to have gone — perhaps to Stair?

Penninghame had 37,300 acres — now 16,000 and Logan Estates have decreased from 16,300 to 10,300 acres. I am surprised that the Monreith estate which belonged to the Maxwells is not mentioned in 1970. It used to be 17,000 acres.

WIGTOWN

Land area	311,984 acres
Inland water	2,892 acres

Estates down to 5,000 acres

Owner	Estates	Acres
Lord Stair	Stair Ests.	105,000
Penninghame Estates	Penninghame Ests.	15,900
Ardwell Estates	Ardwell Ests.	12,300
Logan Garden Trust	Logan Ests.	10,300
David McWhirter	Balminnoch	9,200
Craiglaw Est. Trust	Craiglaw	7,400
Sir A. I. Dunbar	Mochrum	7,100
Unknown	Dunragit	6,400
Milroy Trustees	No name (now sold)	6,300
Tr. of late A. Stewart	Glasserton	5,400

79

Totals of Estates down to 5,000 acres

10 Estates — 185,300 acres

Estates of 5,000 to 1,000 acres

Between			
	5,000 and 4,000 acres:	3:	14,600 acres
	4,000 and 3,000 acres:	6:	22,800 acres
	3,000 and 2,000 acres:	9:	23,800 acres
	2,000 and 1,000 acres:	18;	21,700 acres

Totals of Estates 5,000 to 1,000 acres

36 Estates — 82,900 acres

Summary

Estates over			
	100,000 acres:	1:	105,000 acres
between	20,000 and 10,000 acres:	3:	38,500 acres
	10,000 and 5,000 acres:	6:	41,800 acres
	5,000 and 1,000 acres:	36:	82,900 acres

Grand total of Estates down to 1,000 acres

46 Estates — 268,200 acres

Total land area of county .... 311,984 acres

Total area of private Estates down to 1,000 acres .... 268,200 acres

DUMFRIES

This big county is somewhat better mapped than Ayr, though there are still gaps, rather surprisingly as it has not been much disturbed by mining. Its private ownership in large estates seems to have had a fillip from those flash-in-the-pan forestry groups.

In 1874 Buccleuch was well represented with 265,700 acres (£110,900 including coal). These folk must have had a nose for coal — the only estate in the county to record such income. Today, with 177,700 acres, Buccleuch is still the largest owner by far. The other high fliers seem to have been scared off.

Raehills, once 64,000 is now down to 8,500. But, going up, we have Castlemilk rising from 7,700 acres to 36,000 today. A complete newcomer is the Economic Forestry Group with 32,500 acres.

In the lower bracket it is interesting to find the Mansfields from Scone owning Comlongan, 14,300 acres in 1874. This is reduced, according to the maps to 7,500 acres today — most unlike the Mansfields for this to happen.

80

Springkell also has fallen from 13,400 to 8,500 acres. The Duke of Norfolk appears in this county with 7,500 acres.

Perhaps the most notable present day development here is the emergence of these new catch-penny (in tax relief) forestry finance groups, owning in all 71,400 acres.

DUMFRIES

Land area	688,112 acres
Inland water	4,021 acres

Estates down to 5,000 acres

Owner	Estates	Acres
Duke of Buccleuch	Buccleuch Ests.	177,700
Maj. Buchanan-Jardine	Castlemilk Ests.	35,700
and others	Hoddom	
Economic Forestry Group	Economic Forestry Group	32,500
Trs. I. B. & J. Thomson	Archbank	14,700
Capplegill Ltd.	Capplegill	12,000
Private Forestry Group	Private Forestry Group	10,300
Fountain Forestry Group	Fountain Forestry Group	8,600
Hope-Johnstone Tr.	Raehills	8,500
Lt. Col. Sir J. N. Johnson-Ferguson	Springkell	8,500
Scone Palace Estates (Mansfield)	Comlongan	7,500
Duke of Norfolk	Duke of Norfolk Ests.	7,500
Eliock Estate Co.	Eliock	6,000
Dalswinton Estate Co.	Dalswinton	5,500
Wm. Halliday	Pearsby	5,300
Lady Mary Fitzallan-Howard	Caerlaverock	5,100
Unknown	Weatherlaw	5,100
A. R. Tulloch	Gillesbie	5,000
Tr. E. N. I. Straton-Ferrier	Bonshaw Tower	5,000

Totals of Estates down to 5,000 acres

18 Estates— 360,500 acres

Estates of 5,000 to 1,000 acres

Between			
	5,000 and 4,000 acres:	2:	8,200 acres
	4,000 and 3,000 acres:	4:	13,200 acres
	3,000 and 2,000 acres:	12;	31,200 acres
	2,000 and 1,000 acres:	16:	24,200 acres

Totals of Estates 5,000 to 1,000 acres

34 Estates — 76,800 acres

Summary

Estates over			
	100,000 acres:	1:	177,700 acres
between	40,000 and 30,000 acres:	2:	68,200 acres
	20,000 and 10,000 acres:	3:	37,000 acres
	10,000 and 5,000 acres:	12:	77,600 acres
	5,000 and 1,000 acres:	34:	76,800 acres

81

Grand total of Estates down to 1,000 acres

52 Estates — 437,300 acres

Total land area of county .... 688,112 acres

Total area of private Estates down to 1,000 acres .... 437,300 acres

KIRKCUDBRIGHT

The 1970 maps of the estate boundaries in this large county are extremely strange and quite out of keeping with Millman's splendid work done in most other counties. As a mere 90,000 acres are accounted for out of 574,024, there won't be much to write about. Perhaps this is slightly caused by the fact that the Forestry Commission (in a rough estimate by myself) must own something over 100,000 acres here. As I said earlier, Argyll was the first county 15 years ago in Scotland to reach the target of 100,000 acres planted by the Forestry Commission. Kirkcudbright may have been trying to beat this, and I hope it now leads.

In 1874 there were some huge estates; Mrs Jean Macadam Cathcart of Craigengillan held 39,889 acres with annual value of £5,674 and £58 from lead mines. It is interesting to remember that this lady also held land in Ayr, which brought her annual income from these lands to £23,800 (including coal).

The Callander estate of Falkirk used to own a big chunk of this county — 40,400 acres (£7,600). No trace of this appears today.

The Earl of Galloway however has held on to 10,700 of the 56,000 acres (£7,300) held in 1874, and Cally estate retains 7,400 of its previous 46,000 acres, (£14,600).

Around the period of Millman's survey there was a big change taking place in land speculation and Kirkcudbright seems to have been one of the first counties to be affected. Three private forestry groups are shown as owning a total of almost 30,000 acres of land for forestry.

One other unexpected new owner is the Duke of Norfolk with just over 10,000 acres: thus he owns 17,500 acres in Scotland. We in Scotland should be proud of having the first 'created' Duke (1483) holding so much of our land when in fact he owns 'precious little in his own county' (Masters — 'The Dukes').

82

Land area		574,024 acres
Inland water		6,779 acres

Estates down to 5,000 acres

Owner	Estates	Acres
Economic Forestry Group	Economic Forestry Ests.	11,500
Earl of Galloway	Castle Douglas	10,700
Duke of Norfolk	Duke of Norfolk Ests.	9,600
Mrs E. Murray Usher	Cally Ests.	7,400
Forest Estate Group	Forest Estate	6,900
Private Forestry Group	Private Forestry	6,500
John McC. Scott	Boreland	6,100

Total of Estates down to 5,000 acres

7 Estates — 58,700 acres

Estates of 5,000 to 1,000 acres

Between			
	5,000 and 4,000 acres:	1:	4,000 acres
	4,000 and 3,000 acres:	2:	6,200 acres
	3,000 and 2,000 acres:	5:	12,100 acres
	2,000 and 1,000 acres:	7:	9,300 acres

Totals of Estates 5,000 to 1,000 acres

15 Estates — 31,600 acres

Summary

Estates between			
	20,000 and 10,000 acres:	2:	22,200 acres
	10,000 and 5,000 acres:	5:	36,500 acres
	5,000 and 1,000 acres:	15:	31,600 acres

Grand total of Estates down to 1,000 acres

22 Estates — 90,300 acres

Total land area of county .... 574,024 acres

Total area of private Estates down to 1,000 acres .... 90,300 acres

ROXBURGH

This is the county which has the longest boundary with our English neighbours.

It had, and still has, more than one huge estate, but not quite so huge as in 1874, and there is the loss of the Hirsel's 25,400 acres (£8,000). But Buccleuch's 10,500 acre holding of 1874 has exploded to 60,100 acres, leaving Roxburgh's own Duke to come second with 55,500 acres. They can fight over this discrepancy of around 5,000 acres.

The Marquis of Lothian in 1874 had 19,700 acres (£23,700); he still holds 17,000 acres. Worth what?

Our 1970 list shows 9,000 acres owned by the Tillhill Forestry Group.

I am not sure of the Usher ownership, as Ushers appear in other counties. Is this the booze concern? As a tee-totaller I am concerned to know.

ROXBURGH

Land area	425,564 areas
Inland water	2,440 acres

Estates down to 5,000 acres

Owner	Estates	Acres
Duke of Buccleuch	Buccleuch Ests.	60,100
Duke of Roxburghe	Roxburgh Ests.	55,500
Lord Lothian	Lothian Ests.	17,000
John H. Douglas	Glendearg	10,900
Tillhill Forestry Group	Tillhill Forestry Group	9,000
Andrew Douglas	Saughtree	8,200
Earl of Haddington	Mellerstain	5,200
The Usher Barontcy Tr.	Courthole	5,000
J. M. Elliot	Harwood	5,000

Totals of Estates down to 5,000 acres

9 Estates — 175,900 acres

Estates of 5,000 to 1,000 acres

Between			
5,000 and 4,000 acres:	1:	4,400 acres
4,000 and 3,000 acres:	4:	13,400 acres
3,000 and 2,000 acres:	13:	30,000 acres
2,000 and 1,000 acres:	20:	25,000 acres

Totals of Estates 5,000 to 1,000 acres

38 Estates — 72,800 acres

Summary

Estates between			
75,000 and 50,000 acres:	2:	115,600 acres
20,000 and 10,000 acres:	2:	27,900 acres
10,000 and 5,000 acres:	5:	32,400 acres
5,000 and 1,000 acres:	38:	72,800 acres

Grand total of Estates down to 5,000 acres

47 Estates — 248,700 acres

Total land area of county .... 424,564 acres

Total area of private Estates down to 1,000 acres .... 248,700 acres

Summary of Estates down to 1,000 acres in the South

In Thousands

COUNTY	100+		100/75		75/50		50/40		40/30		30/20		20/10		10/5		5/1	
	Est.	Acres	Est.	Acres	Est.	Acres	Est.	Acres	Est.	Acres	Est.	Acres	Est.	Acres	Est.	Acres	Est.	Acres
CLACKMANNAN	—	—	—	—	—	—	—	—	—	—	—	—	—	—	1	5.0	12	21.8
KINROSS	—	—	—	—	—	—	—	—	—	—	—	—	—	—	—	—	9	18.4
FIFE	—	—	—	—	—	—	—	—	—	—	—	—	—	—	8	48.4	33	62.9
DUMBARTON	—	—	—	—	—	—	—	—	—	—	—	—	—	—	—	—	29	60.6
STIRLING	—	—	—	—	—	—	1	42.7	—	—	—	—	1	10.2	4	28.6	55	104.9
W. LOTHIAN	—	—	—	—	—	—	—	—	—	—	—	—	—	—	—	—	17	37.9
MIDLOTHIAN	—	—	—	—	—	—	—	—	—	—	—	—	3	34.3	4	26.5	27	56.3
E. LOTHIAN	—	—	—	—	—	—	—	—	—	—	—	—	1	13.0	3	20.6	26	42.2
RENFREW	—	—	—	—	—	—	—	—	—	—	—	—	1	10.8	2	12.0	17	36.3
LANARK	—	—	—	—	—	—	1	48.0	—	—	2	43.0	1	11.0	2	12.7	28	58.0
PEEBLES	—	—	—	—	—	—	—	—	—	—	2	50.5	2	28.2	7	43.1	18	41.5
SELKIRK	—	—	—	—	—	—	—	—	—	—	—	—	—	—	1	6.5	18	40.9
BERWICK	—	—	—	—	—	—	—	—	—	—	—	—	1	12.9	11	76.8	34	70.6
AYR	—	—	—	—	—	—	—	—	—	—	—	—	3	46.1	8	63.1	31	61.8
WIGTOWN	1	105.0	—	—	—	—	—	—	2	68.2	—	—	3	38.5	6	41.8	36	82.9
DUMFRIES	1	177.7	—	—	—	—	—	—	—	—	—	—	3	37.0	12	77.6	34	76.8
KIRCUDBRIGHT	—	—	—	—	2	115.6	—	—	—	—	—	—	2	22.2	5	36.5	15	31.6
ROXBURGH	—	—	—	—	—	—	—	—	—	—	—	—	2	27.9	5	32.4	38	72.8
TOTALS	2	282.7	—	—	2	115.6	2	90.7	2	68.2	4	93.5	23	292.1	79	531.6	480	978.2

Number of Estates and Acreages for each Region

Size Categories (Acres)/(In Thousands)	WEST		N.E.		SOUTH		TOTALS	
	Ests.	Acres	Ests.	Acres	Ests.	Acres	Ests.	Acres
100,000+	3	339.4	1	130.0	2	282.7	6	752.1
100,000/75,000	5	433.8	1	75.0	—	—	6	508.8
75,000/50,000	15	918.3	5	297.2	2	115.6	22	1331.1
50,000/40,000	13	559.8	4	177.6	2	90.7	19	828.1
40,000/30,000	15	513.2	5	171.2	2	68.2	22	752.6
30,000/20,000	30	643.4	12	281.3	4	93.5	46	1018.2
20,000/10,000	95	1408.2	57	765.6	23	292.1	175	2465.9
10,000/5,000	102	706.9	69	462.8	79	531.6	250	1701.3
5,000/1,000	258	630.4	455	1063.6	480	978.2	1193	2672.2
	536	6153.4	609	3424.3	594	2452.6	1739	12030.3

Summary of
Private Estates in the Three Regions

In Thousands

REGION	100+ Est.	Acres	100/75 Est.	Acres	75/50 Est.	Acres	50/40 Est.	Acres	40/30 Est.	Acres	30/20 Est.	Acres	20/10 Est.	Acres	10/5 Est.	Acres	5/1 Est.	Acres
CROFTING COUNTIES AND BUTE	3	339.4	5	433.8	15	918.3	13	559.8	15	513.2	30	643.4	95	1408.2	102	706.9	258	630.4
N. EAST AND PERTHSHIRE	1	130.0	1	75.0	5	297.2	4	177.6	5	171.2	12	281.3	57	765.6	69	462.8	455	1063.6
SOUTH	2	282.7	—		2	115.6	2	90.7	2	68.2	4	93.5	23	292.1	79	531.6	480	978.2
TOTALS	6	752.1	6	508.8	22	1331.1	19	828.1	22	752.6	46	1018.2	175	2465.9	250	1701.3	1193	2672.2

Final Summary for Regions

Regions	Estates	Acres
West	536	6,153,400
N.E.	609	3,424,300
South	594	2.452,600
	1,739	12,030,300

FINAL SUMMARY FOR ALL SCOTLAND

Private Estates: their numbers, and acreages within size Categories

Estates of	100,000 acres	upwards			6:	752,100	acres
Estates between	100,000	and	75,000	acres	6:	508,800	acres
,,	75,000	,,	50,000	,,	22:	1,331,100	,,
,,	50,000	,,	40,000	,,	19:	828,100	,,
,,	40,000	,,	30,000	,,	22:	752,600	,,
,,	30,000	,,	20,000	,,	46:	1,018,200	,,
,,	20,000	,,	10,000	,,	175:	2,465,900	,,
,,	10,000	,,	5,000	,,	250:	1,701,300	,,
,,	5,000	,,	1,000	,,	1193:	2,672,200	,,

Grand total of private Estates down to 1,000 acres

1,739 Estates — 12,030,300 acres

Total land area of Scotland ....19,068,807 acres

Total area of private Estates down to 1,000 acres ....12,030,300 acres

Management And Husbandry
Of Our Land

Private Enterprise in Forestry

Having now stated the facts relating to the break-up of land in Scotland into private estates in size from Buccleuch's obscene 277,000 acres down to those around the 1,000 mark, there is now presented a clear and fairly accurate picture of the extent to which private ownership of land can and does determine our way of life. We also know the very minor share of responsibility left in the hands of the ordinary citizen, when it is realised that we, as citizens, own a mere 2.5 per cent of the land in Scotland.

Now that the actual ownership of land has been completed I shall go on to describe as briefly and succinctly as possible the management, by private enterprise, of this valuable asset — land — but before doing so I am going to digress as I wish to show how light-heartedly present-day owners treat their land business.

In 1976 the BBC, with the seeming objective of letting the public know something about land and its uses, gave us on television a tale of three estates, two in Perthshire and one in Ross-shire, and their main interests. The Ross-shire one was that of Sir John Stirling's 10,000 acres at Fairburn where the best part of the day must have been spent following the landlord and his stalker crawling on their bellies, finally shooting a hind stone-dead. The ending was a display of the estate staff from the burly game-keeper down to the house-maid, in a long straight line in front of the big house. The one at Blair Castle, the 130,000 acres holding of the Duke of Atholl, was exactly the same, a similar crawling with a dead deer at the end of the long journey. However, the finale was quite different, a complete march-past led by pipers of the Duke's very own private army of Atholl Highlanders.

The other one in Perthshire, with Chris Brasher in charge, was brief. Lord Mansfield, a keen blood-sportsman but with no deer forest, was unable to show his skill with the rifle. A much more paternal affair: the loading of the hay waggon and finally, like

90

Fairburn, a rather longer line of his faithfuls headed by the Laird himself and his game-keeper downwards. I think I should record the ending of this broadcast. It made its way quickly through Scotland down to Wales where some considerable time must have been spent and with a good deal more bite in its showing up of some of the autocratic arrogance of the typical British landlord towards farm workers and others. There must have been a slip-up somewhere, which means that I shall require to be careful, as the end was a Court case with fines and costs totalling £50,000 .

Estate management is a very tricky business. To get the full potential out of land of any quality is a difficult and highly skilled job of work and, as in any other business, in two directions, finance and husbandry. The usual routine is a combination of landlord and factor, the latter sitting tight on the Estate and always very much the junior partner. Being an estate factor is one of the most insecure jobs in any industry: at the mercy of the whims of the most unpredictable class of men. Factors are here today and away tomorrow, in the main an able lot, with some of them wizards in financial matters concerning taxation on land and so on. One such told me that he spotted a weakness in some aspect of tax which enabled the estate to save hefty sums. This has been going on for generations but very much on the quiet. Then in the early 1960s there appeared the first of these finance forestry groups, Economic Forestry Group (E.F.G.) with a Scotsman, K. N. Rankin, C.A. in charge. At the British Association for the Advancement of Science annual meeting in Dundee in 1968 he declared quite openly and bluntly from the platform that his Group would not plant a single tree if it were not for the "helpful tax structure and the generous Forestry Commission grants". The long-time-well-kept secrecy by private estates of tax relief was blown sky high, and became public property with the pressure then building up on the government to do something about it. Denis Healey had to do something, and he tried hard but it takes a lang spoon to sup with our landlord system and we are now back almost where we were. That is the work of the estate factors. They are clever in that line of work.

But there are clever landlords as well. I knew one, for whom I did a lot of forestry work, a very able, wealthy, good manager of extensive farm land (but not forestry) who told me he had never paid income tax in his life and never would. He is gone to his long rest now. I wonder if he ever did pay tax or was he pulling my leg?

91

G

When it comes down to field work the cleverness seems to depart, and as we have been discussing forestry I shall continue on this subject and show what private enterprise has done, over the years, in this vital industry.

In the past thirty years or so we have had two censuses of private woodlands very thoroughly carried out by the Forestry Commission (F.C.), one in 1947-49 and a less detailed one in 1965-67.

The results of the 1947-49 census were tragic and there was very little, if any, improvement shown in the second one. I shall deal entirely with the first, as I was concerned with it in Perthshire, Angus and parts of Kincardine and Fife.

Woodlands (the broad term) are classified as (a) productive and (b) unproductive. The total acreage of private woodlands was in 1947-49 1,024,000 acres of which 650,000 acres were in this census classified as unproductive leaving a mere 374,000 acres as a growing crop, much of which was in a poor condition. Thirty-seven per cent productive woodland; 63 per cent bare, unproductive.

Further proof of this poor miserly management was made as the result of an enquiry by the late Professor H. M. Steven into the production of the felling of 230,000 acres of private woodlands during the late war (State-owned plantations had not reached the stage of being ready to fell). H. M. Steven, of Aberdeen University, in charge of field operations under the Board of Trade, was able to show that production was a mere 1675 cubic feet per acre when this should have been not less than 5000 to 6000. During both world wars I was in the middle of timber production and the position in the first one was equally bad. In both we had to scrape the bottom of the barrel for every cubic foot.

Another aspect of this easy-going attitude on the part of our landlords (England is no better) is their carelessness towards the generous (Rankin's expression) Forestry Commission grants for planting and management of new plantations; and this was very clearly shown-up when two of our local nobility with very large estates had to refund up to £3,000 between them for bad husbandry. How much of this bad husbandry has escaped is anyone's guess as the above two cases took place during the period of the 1964 Labour Government when overseeing private planting, heavily subsidised by public money, began to bite.

The dependence of private forestry on tax relief and F.C. grants is very clearly shown in Graph no. 2. In the late 1960s, when the half dozen Forestry Groups began to operate, private planting soared from 15,000 acres per annum to 42,000 and then again dropped to 22,000 on the threat of Transfer Tax and the actual reduction in the size of F.C. grants. Planting grants have now (April 1977) been more than doubled — from £18 per acre to £40.50, with the very considerable added inducement of £3 per acre per annum for management grant. Planting for 1977 will not be affected but it may and probably will soar again in 1978, and for all this Government financial assistance and tax relief, all timber at the end of the day belongs entirely to the landlord. So, Denis Healey's bite has not gone very deep. Very much more could be written about the almost complete failure of private landlordism in the important industry of forestry, insofar as Scotland is concerned, but for the purpose of this book what I have stated should suffice, except to remark that in Perthshire here I am surrounded by large estates such as Lansdowne, Murthly, Atholl, Mansfield, Grandtully where their forestry has been going at half-cock, and others such as Meggernie (Wills) where it is practically non-existent — all land top grade for growing trees able, under good management, to produce up to 10,000 cubic feet of first class timber and in a short rotation of 40 years or slightly less.

The Forestry Commission

The formation of the Forestry Commission (F.C.) in 1919 with the objective of establishing state-owned forests was one of the finest things which ever happened in land ownership and land use in Britain. The reason for this move is not far to seek: the complete failure in private forestry to produce timber for war-time emergency, but equally essential, for everyday domestic use.

I have in front of me the first Annual Report of the Commission for year 1919-1920. In it a brief resumé is given of the state of the industry. A paragraph on page 7 sums it up: "In reviewing this period of private forestry it must be admitted that continuity of management — so essential in forestry — was conspicuous by its absence." A point I have kept hammering. A further quote: "There was no state organisation, little state assistance in planting and no education or research. The woods were not even planted for commercial purposes, a large proportion being created for scenic effect, sport or shelter. In a word, the private owner, while conscientiously endeavouring to provide for social rural requirements (farm buildings, vehicles, fencing etc.), for game cover and amenity, was unable from the circumstances of the case, to provide against the unforeseen increase in the consumption of softwood timber which was one of the results of the enormous increase in industrialisation in the U.K. in the Nineteenth Century." And, furthermore, for the 1914 and 1939 wars.

From 1885, committee after committee had been set up to go into this question of commercial tree-growing and nothing happened. The 1914 war, however, brought matters to a head. I quote again: "In 1916 the people were hungry, yet despite the most strenuous efforts to set more ships free for imported grain, it was found impossible to reduce even by 1 per cent the proportion of shipping required to carry the timber required essential for war operations abroad and at home. Napoleon's maxim that an army marches on its belly had to be brought up to date. . . . In 1916 Mr Asquith appointed a subcommittee of the Reconstruction Committee of the Cabinet under the chairmanship of Mr F. D. Acland to consider and report upon the best means of conserving and developing the woodland and forestry resources of the kingdom having regard to the experience gained during the war." I have never seen the Acland Report (I would very much like to) though it has rung through my ears for well over 60 years.

It was presented in May 1917 laying down broad principles on which a national policy should be based and was accepted by the Cabinet. An Interim Forestry Authority set up in 1918 was followed on 20 November 1919 by the establishment of the Forestry Commission — a notable date in the mind and diary of every forester.

I have also got 'The Forestry Act of 1919' in front of me. It is divided into 11 sections and I shall extract for my purpose those parts which highlight its main objectives:—

Section 3: In this it is stated that the Commissioners (eight were appointed — see later note) shall have power:

(i) To acquire land for afforestation and manage, plant, erect buildings etc. on such land.

(ii) Establish and carry on, or aid, in the establishment of woodland industries.

(iii) Promote forestry education and forestry publications.

(iv) Carry out research.

94

(v) Help private forestry.

Section 4: Control vermin — rabbits and hares, squirrels — on their own and private owners' land.

Section 7: . . . "apply to the Development Commissioners for an order empowering them to acquire land compulsorily".

Of the eight members of the first Commission, four were large land owners (3 Scottish, 1 English) under the chairmansip of Lord Lovat.

Over the past 58 years the Commission, with its continuous acquisition of quite extensive areas of land, has all along had hostility shown to it by private landlords with the ever recurring barbed shaft of "a back-door to the nationalisation of land". However, in the appointment of Lord Lovat as its first chairman (and he held on to this important post for seven years) landlords knew that in this able, arrogant, domineering man they had someone in charge who, when he got this completely new young organisation within his claws, would see to it that, as a Government department, it would never overreach itself and get out of hand. This has proved to be the case up to the present day.

In those 58 years, apart from a short spell when R. L. Robinson, ex-Australian, professional forester (who was no favourite with private landlords) chaired, one big landowner after another took charge until Lord Waldegrave resigned in 1964, when major changes were made in the composition of the Commission.

Instead of 10 part-time Commissioners the new set-up consists of 4 full-time civil servant Commissioners, 3 of them F.C. employees, and 6 part-time ones, of whom, with a salary of around £5,000, one is chairman. Part-time Commissioners are paid out-of-pocket expenses, with a five-year stint. The first new style chairman, L. A. Jenkins, was connected with the timber trade; he was followed by Tom Taylor, ex-head of the Scottish Co-operative Society, Glasgow (Lord Taylor of Gryfe and a socialist); he stepped down in 1976 and, looking back on his term of office, the oustanding feature of it was the extreme support he gave to private estate forestry. A reference to this, I think, excessive help, was made in Scottish Woodlands Owners' annual report of 1974-75 where under the bold heading "APPRECIATION" it was stated that "the private sector (forestry) owes more to Lord Taylor than will probably ever be publicly known". He has just signed the 56th Annual F.C. Report, and we await the 57th under the signature of the new chairman, John Mackie, farmer/landowner, socialist, ex-Joint Parliamentary

Secretary at the Ministry of Agriculture, Fisheries and Food (MAFF) from 1964 to 1970. He has, jointly with another Fabian, written a pamphlet favouring land nationalisation. Let's hope something big and really worth while comes out of his five-year term. There is much need.

As a strong advocate of nationalised industries, I wonder if it is strange that I have always envied the men with power, as Commissioners, at the top of this State-owned industry. I suppose it is too late now, but I reckon I could have put some fire into the belly of this body concerned with the use of land for tree-growing. One of the curses of State industries up to the present is the fact that dedicated men, left-wing socialists if you like, so rarely get into the seats of power and thus prove that private enterprise is left far behind. Even without such men at the top, the Forestry Commission, with all its failings and they are many, has just done that.

This applies particularly to work in the field where the F.C. leads the world in the establishment of young plantations, for example in plant nursery work where Alex Rose (an ex-apprentice of mine), forester-in-charge, perfected a miracle plant lining-out machine which cut out the slavish work of a countless number of men and women crawling all day on their knees on the ground. It also applies to research, in which we now have two excellent stations, one at the Bush near Edinburgh, and one at Alice Holt, south of London — both carrying a terrific load of work. Some of the men I have known in this branch have been outstanding, and in this regard I think of my old friend Mark L. Anderson, by far the ablest, high-ranking forester in British forestry, but one whom the Colonel Blimps in charge of the Commission could not tolerate. He took up a senior post in the Irish Free State, but rejoined the F.C. within two years. I followed him to Ireland, but had to leave for family health reasons before three years were up. Anderson followed me and got to the top in the Irish Forestry Service. I was in line for this if I had remained. He left Ireland for the second time and his last ten years were in Edinburgh as Professor of Forestry in the University where he produced his colossal two-volume work "Scottish Forestry". I mention Anderson to show up the attitude of the top men who kept this brilliant forester from serving his whole life in British forestry with the Forestry Commission. Despite this, some most important pieces of research such as that of D. G. Pyatt on poor pan-bound soils on the extensive areas of our heath land (proving that extra deep ploughing was required before trees can be planted), have been completed.

The various ups and downs of the Forestry Commission in its 58 years have been frequent, and often quite serious. In the early '20s there was the big reduction in senior staff by the "Geddes axe", then in the depressed period in the early 1930s millions of plants had to be destroyed. In my mind, however, the most serious crisis occurred in the 1970s when Heath's despicable Government seemed determined to blot out the Commission altogether, when the annual acquisition of land came down in 1970-71 from almost 50,000 acres to a mere 10,000 in 1973-74, when the price of land in the same period (see graph) rocketed from under £20 in 1970 to £110 in 1975-76. The Labour Government just came in time in 1974 to save the situation.

Changes in Governments have had very serious effects in Scotland. In 1964 when the Tories were defeated they had planned a very much reduced annual planting programme of around 21,000 acres. As soon as Willie Ross (with all his faults in my opinion the finest Secretary of State for Scotland we have ever had) took over, he increased this to 30,000, soon after to 36,000 acres and just before Labour went out in 1971 to 50,000. I keep wondering if Scotsmen ever think about how much is gained by having a Labour Government in power. Fifty thousand acres of state-owned land being developed every year under trees by Labour against 10,000 or even none by a Tory Government. Just as with top management in State industry, to which I have already referred, in relation to full production, the very same applies to political control from the top; Tories in power doing their damnedest, as in State forestry, to hinder, Labour in power trying their utmost, against terrific odds, to bring success.

Forestry Education & Careers

The Forestry Commission's outlook on education has been a most unhappy one. We in Scotland have been well equipped, perhaps over-equipped, in higher University education, with two universities offering degrees in forestry. For the ordinary working forester, when the F.C. was started off there was no normal run-of-the-mill college education in forestry such as there was in the three Agricultural Colleges in agriculture. The F.C. set up their own schools, miserable, miserly affairs to which I took exception, increasingly so the more I saw of them. I kept pressing for similar facilities to those offered to agricultural workers. When Anderson took over forestry in Edinburgh University he responded to this pressure (he told me so later) and tried out a course in forestry between his own department and the East of Scotland Agricultural College, which in its early history had one and two-year courses in forestry, but Anderson's effort failed owing mainly to the fact that he got no support from the Forestry Commission, but also to the fact that amongst all the educationalists in forestry in the universities and colleges and the professional societies there was not one single individual, except Professor Mark L. Anderson, with the vision to support me in the demand for a School of Forestry jointly for degree men and diploma men (O.H.D. and H.N.D.). Today in Scotland, although we have, as working foresters, led in this field since the 1880s, there is no worthwhile education for working foresters. This is a dreadful reflection on our Forestry Commission's treatment of its own and private estate foresters, in not supplementing the practical work of these men with an advanced education, thus equipping them to more than hold their own against the inexperienced degree men. Only these varsity chaps can get to the top, and as a result, the Commission has in its 55 years been a massive loser.

Before I leave this aspect of education and a career with the commission, may I make a few comments on my own personal experience with this Department of State. I was warned more than once to watch my step where politics were concerned and to go easy. I am afraid I did not take much notice of this advice from some of my closest friends. Even Lord Lovat warned me, when I was in London once at a promotion selection board for District Officer vacancies, "not to be so damned independent" if I wished to make a career with the Commission. Strangely enough, I was promoted a year or two later — in 1928. Lovat was gone by that time. Promotion did not bring me any financial improvement, but it did give me the chance of getting to the top — I was then in the officer grade. At the time I had a salary of £210 plus house and garden. In Wales I had £300 and no house. However, the top grade of forester-in-charge today is very much better off, with a salary in the region of £6,000 plus house and probably, if you are not very ambitious, by far the most desirable forestry job in the country. However, foresters-in-charge have to wear that abomination — a uniform. I just refused point blank. Perhaps it is not surprising that in those early days I was considered the "enfant terrible" and today "that old so-and-so". I won't get time to live it down.

I must now deal briefly with one or two quite important items.

The Commission's Failures

Between 1920 and 1924 the F.C. was paying its workers around 45/- per week. This "high" wage did not suit the finances of the private estate owner and great pressure was brought on the F.C. to reduce — perhaps it did not take much to effect a change. In any event I was told to pay something under 40/- and I just refused to do so, and as far as I remember when I left the north 40/- was the wage I was still paying. Wages later came down drastically for all the Commission's field workers. There was no trade union.

The 1919 Forestry Act gave the F.C. powers to set up processing plant — pulp mills, sawmills — to manufacture their own timber. Up to date (1977) nothing has happened: instead the timber trade "lame ducks" were helped along. Various examples prove this point. A sum of £15,000 was lent to Messrs Wilson, Timber Merchants, Troon, for the erection of a sawmill and seasoning plant at Strachur, Lochfyne, to process State-grown timber. Then at Fort William the multinational firm, Wiggins Teape & Co. Ltd., got stuck with the erection of their pulp mill when they had spent £10 million. A Government loan of £10 million was given with the condition that no interest would be paid until the business was showing a profit. I have often wondered how long this period of "no profit" lasted. Here again the timber supplied was mainly State-grown, much of it of a size fit for the sawmill and far too valuable for pulp. I repeat, processing of its own timber must be carried out by the Commission.

The Commission was also given powers to acquire land compulsorily but has never used them. The day of complacency regarding using these powers is long past. John Mackie must see to it that the annual planting programme for the next 20 years is not less than 50,000 acres per annum — whatever more — and that at the end of the day in Scotland we have two million acres per annum on a rotation of 40 years, and private estate forestry of one million acres, helped by the Government only if the high standard of 200 cubic feet per acre per annum is produced.

One final note — on game and the Commission's complete failure to take advantage of the powers given to them in the 1919 Act to "control" this menace. In fact they themselves have even entered into this "ugly" (Heath's word) blood-sports business, in red deer and perhaps grouse. As citizens of a so-called civilised country, let's give it up on our own land, and let us as well control the invasion of these pests from private estates.

The Commission has now been in existence for 58 years. I sincerely hope it does not last much longer, as its structure is entirely wrong. It should be run exactly the same as the very much larger and more important Ministry of Agriculture (we have no Ministry of Forestry) with no outsiders interfering with a new, independent civil service-run forestry organisation — call it what you will.

Postscript

I have just recalled an incident belonging to the beginning of the Forestry Commission, which I think is worth recording. It happened around 1924-25 when a week's field conference was planned and carried out on Commission forests in the Fort Augustus area. There were about 15 of us (I cannot recall everyone) made up of top men — three Commissioners, then the officers — divisional and district — followed by the N.C.O.s, ordinary forest grade, of which I was one. Of the two hotels in Fort Augustus the larger and perhaps more posh one was occupied by the three Commissioners — alone. The other smaller, quite decent, but perhaps less posh one, was taken over by the officers and foresters, the former having individual bedrooms, the latter sharing rooms. Officers and foresters were kept away from each other at meals and had no contact whatever in the hotel.

That was Lovat's army procedure. Could that possibly happen today with Taylor of Gryfe or John Mackie? We have made progress but we must go much further.

GRAPH 1

FORESTRY COMMISSION LAND PRICES

£3 IN 1919 TO £110 IN 1974—£52 IN 1976 (p. acre)

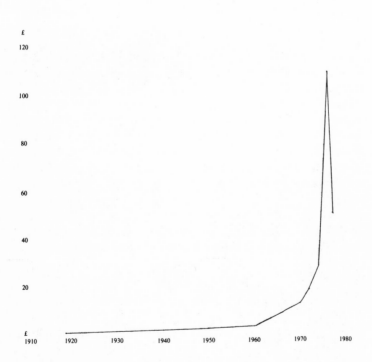

101

GRAPH 2

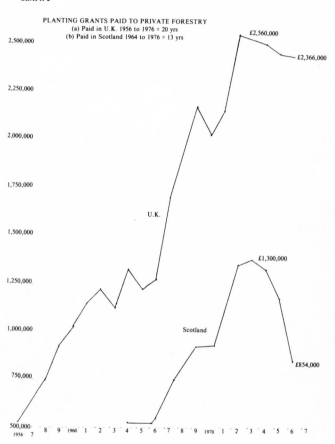

PLANTING GRANTS PAID TO PRIVATE FORESTRY
(a) Paid in U.K. 1956 to 1976 = 20 yrs
(b) Paid in Scotland 1964 to 1976 = 13 yrs

£2,560,000

£2,366,000

2,500,000

2,250,000

2,000,000

1,750,000

U.K.

1,500,000

£1,300,000

1,250,000

Scotland

1,000,000

£854,000

750,000

500,000
1956 7   8   9 1960 1   2   3   4   5   6   7   8   9 1970 1   2   3   4   5   6   7

GRAPH 3

Scotland

PRIVATE ESTATE PLANTING
20 years 1956-1976

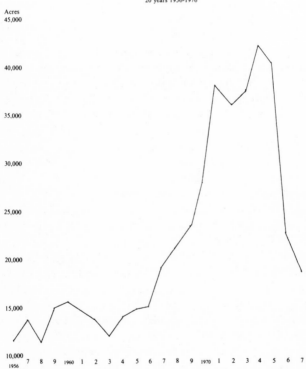

Acres
45,000

40,000

35,000

30,000

25,000

20,000

15,000

10,000
1956 7 8 9 1960 1 2 3 4 5 6 7 8 9 1970 1 2 3 4 5 6 7

103

Private Enterprise in Agriculture

My brief survey of forestry brought out the inefficiency of private landlordism. The fact that our agriculture is more or less under the same management must influence any statement of mine regarding its adequacy. That is, I may be biased — I probably am. As I do not know as much about agriculture as I do of forestry, I shall, besides stating my own opinion, bring in expert agriculturists.

In the May 1975 issue of 'Scottish Farming' there appeared an up-to-date U.K. survey — by experts — of the major operations in agriculture, stock-rearing, cereal-growing, machinery use, drainage and so on. This survey revealed that the colossal sum of £900,000,000 was lost annually through poor management. Scotland, presumably, would account for £243,000,000 of this loss.

Our agricultural area is roughly 13,000,000 acres, 4 millions of which are 'arable' and 9 millions 'upland'.

As I travelled over Scotland engaged in forestry I have all along kept a very close watch on agriculture wherever I have been. My own estimate of the quality of husbandry, over all, is that, in the 'arable' areas productivity is around 80 per cent of its potential, whereas in the huge 'upland' or marginal land area it barely reaches the 50 per cent mark. I have studied 'Agricultural Statistics 1975 Scotland' and 'Scottish Agricultural Economics 1976' closely. They give us many — very many figures (e.g.1,349,498 hens are listed), but, as no information is anywhere available on land *capability* we are again forced to form our own estimates. Discussions I have had with Agricultural College advisers have confirmed my own estimates of loss through bad husbandry. I discussed these estimates quite recently with Edwin Lawson, son of a small Aberdeenshire farmer, who after working on the land trained as an engineer and later worked with Bisset of Blairgowrie, farm machinery engineers and inventors, as their agent, travelling all over Scotland.

He agreed with my estimate of the misuse of 'upland' areas, but thought that the 'arable' section would be producing 85 per cent of its potential. He, however, stressed that adjoining farms on best quality land were producing different results. One (because of poor drainage or neglect) might be going back to the wild while its neighbour was reaching 90 per cent of its potential. In view of this I think I may hold on to an 80 per cent estimate.

The loss of 20 per cent production on our 4 millions acres of top grade land is no laughing matter.

Behind the high dykes surrounding many of out stately homes lies a surprisingly large section of the cream of our agricultural land, retained simply to give our owners the privacy they demand.

The following are a few examples:
Drummond Castle and South Esk (Kinnaird Castle), each with around 2,000 acres.
Glamis and Scone Palace — each around 500 acres — Scone possibly has the finest site in Britain.

By going all over Scotland we could find at least half a million of these carefully guarded acres. No-one is likely to believe this splendid land is seriously used for agriculture. In some cases, certainly, there are ornamental sheep, cattle, ponies, deer, peacocks even giraffes and camels enjoying the pasture.

The use of the uplands and rough grazing areas as a playground for blood sportsmen accounts for the huge loss we estimated there.

The 'Highland Forum' (a body of owners, factors and others) in its 1968 report of its examination of land use, declared ". . . it was thought undesirable that so many owners still looked upon their land as a sporting playground for their own selfish amusement, and that this often meant misuse of the land itself in order to make it a better wilderness for wild life. Land ownership should be deemed a trust and where the owner cannot see this, the Government should forcibly intervene".

So there are some reasonable owners too, though in the same paragraph they were stating that "private ownership was preferable to State" because of the *loving care* and personal interest shown by the private owner.

At the International Bio-meteorological Congress in 1975, John Bryden of the Highlands and Islands area, commented, "Although it covers nearly half the surface area of Scotland it produces but one tenth of the estimated gross output of agriculture, forestry and game in Scotland . . ." and there has been a *relative decline* in the contribution of the region to primary production in Scotland in the past century and a half. This is not good enough.

In Perthshire (within our N.E. region), on Loch Tayside we have thousands of acres, at one time given the beautiful name of the 'garden of Breadalbane', now entirely under sheep, and so degraded as to be carrying only 1 sheep to 2½ acres, and, in humans, one family per 2,000 acres. Not less than 50 per cent of this land should be back in tillage, while the other half should be so improved as to carry one sheep to the acre, and the whole should be providing a comfortable living for ten times as many families as at present. From John O'Groats to the Borders the picture is repeated and repeated and repeated.

Some landlords have stated to me quite frankly that they were fencing off some of their good grass land to try to bring back heather — and grouse. On neighbouring estates, owners are warning progressive tenants to discontinue hill-ploughing and re-seeding which would have produced more valuable grazing for their sheep.

Is it surprising that our 9,000,000 acres of rough grazing are producing so little?

Aids for Agriculture

It is terrific the amount of help meted out to our landlords, farmers, crofters, horticulturalists, by Government departments etc. and, in the main, paid for by you and me.

In Scotland by far the biggest body of workers in this direction is that of the Department of Agriculture and Fisheries for Scotland (DAFS) with its headquarters in St Andrew's House, Edinburgh, and its 30 area and local offices all over Scotland, from Lerwick to Benbecula down to Stranraer, responsible for paying out around £63,000,000 annually, in subsidies and grants. The services offered by this department cannot be measured or valued. How many research stations are carried on by it? I have not tried to find out, but of this I am sure: agriculturists of every standing, with few exceptions, are dragging their feet far behind research work being carried out and completed by these forward-looking department men and women.

If our practising farmers were as advanced we would not be struggling and paying such prices as we are today for our grub, but the middle-man would have to be eliminated so as to get to rock bottom value.

Then we have the agricultural colleges, again covering the whole of Scotland and advising more directly in every aspect of agriculture and horticulture. Like the department men, their advice and help are of inestimable value. I have had close contacts with them for many years. In 1931 or thereabouts I was in a Forestry Commission smallholding of about two acres being guided by Mr Wilson of West of Scotland Agricultural College in Oban. There, certainly on a very limited patch, I grew 14 tons per acre of Golden Wonder potatoes. Everywhere I have been since, it is a joy to meet these advisers and get their help. I am sure farmers and landowners can back me up in this.

There is one further body of advisers who are carrying out outstanding but more specialised work and I refer to the men with the Hill Farming Research Organisation, men who, if given the chance, would change the face of our dreich, blae hill and marginal lands, not merely in the Highlands but all over Scotland. In Perthshire alone we have not less than 500,000 acres of such lands just waiting to be handled by H.F.R.O. to let the world know that we are actually alive. I should think they could cross the border and help in England and Wales as well. Some day, and I hope very soon, we shall be joining together as U.K. citizens much more closely on this vital question of getting the full potential out of these important, neglected hill lands.

I am not writing further on this new research body but I am going to take advantage of my friend Gordon Brown and quote from the "Red Paper" what Dr Cunningham of H.F.R.O. said in an address at the British Association in Stirling in 1974. This stuff is just right up my street and needs no comment from me:

"There are some who regard the Highland region as little more than a wilderness and consider that agriculture, especially hill-farming is of no consequence (and should be substantially abandoned). We may be discussing an underdeveloped area, but certainly not one in which the spectre of starvation haunts the inhabitants, but rather one which could make an increasing contribution to the national larder for the teeming millions packed in the S.E. of England. The view has been expressed that the Highland area is the only unspoilt region in Europe and should be kept in its present state. This implies that the presence of man and agriculture is in some way undesirable, and this I would question."

H

Little Neddies

Since writing the above chapter, I have received the publications (June '77) of the Agricultural E.D.C. ('Little Neddy') entitled 'Agriculture into the 1980s'. I quote some of the findings of this authoritative body:

(1) "There is room for significant increases in productivity . . . based on the . . . soils, situations . . . equipment, agrochemicals, skills and knowledge we already have. . . . The basis of this argument is the great disparity which at present exists between (comparable) high-yielding and low-yielding farms."

(2) "That progress has been achieved in the past is due, in no small measure, to the positive approach of the labour force."

(3) "Man-management, as in other industries, is of increasing importance . . . many farmers find difficulties in getting away for mid-career management courses . . . provided by the Agriculture Training Board."

(4) "Losses in productivity arising from the failure to apply proven technology at farm level . . . are, by any standard, *large*."

In the six books so far produced, 'Little Neddy' has not mentioned game as an agricultural pest, and the only reference I can find to landlordism is in a brief footnote suggesting nationalisation as a possible way out of farming difficulties.

I am very glad to be able to add this official, deeply researched confirmation of what I have seen with my own eyes over many decades.

The Swann Report

Alongside of these recent studies carried out by the various N.E.D.C. (Neddy) Committees we have also the Swann Report, the result of enquiry, chaired by Sir Michael Swann, by a committee of thirteen with assistance from over 400 U.K. bodies and individuals plus evidence from over 200 organisations and individuals "visited by the Committee", all over the world.

This enquiry went deeply and specifically into the health and welfare of farm livestock and brought out the fact that in the U.K. the veterinary profession, in all its aspects, academic, public research, private practice and so on, was far from satisfied with the health and welfare of farm livestock in Scotland and the losses which ensued. I am making no comment and I have already expressed my opinion. Instead I am quoting from the "Appenders to Report", a couple of sentences on page 60, which I consider to be the operative words covering the whole report: "However, in a free market economy it is by no means certain that the reduction or elimination of losses followed by expansion would result in higher returns for farmers — it would depend on the extent to which prices reacted to changing supplies of particular products. These considerations are omitted in this report, but it should be emphasised that irrespective of the impact of reduced losses on farmers' production and returns the reduction of losses involved in livestock would add a note to the sum total of human welfare."

These "Little Neddy" reports are indispensable for anyone interested in land use in Scotland — they certainly cover the U.K. but that makes no difference. The first one on Grass and grass products, published in 1974 deals with U.K. farming and the Common Market. The next five, published between April and June 1977 with the general heading of "Agriculture into the 1980s", deal with Land Use, Resources and Strategy, Animal Feeding Stuffs, Manpower, Taxation, and Finance. I wish I had had them earlier as each one goes to prove in one way and another that we are not by any means getting the full potential out of our precious asset — land.

The same applies to the terrific coverage of the Swann report and, again, I wish I had known it earlier, but I am not an agriculturist, only a mere forester with a deep concern in the use of our land in agriculture as well as forestry.

Game

Landlords are often seen to play down the use they make of their land as a private playground. The late Sir John Stirling Maxwell was frank. He wrote: "It may be true, I believe it often is, that a deer forest employs more people than the same area under sheep. It certainly brings in a larger rent. From a purely parochial point of view it may therefore claim to be economically sound: but from no other. It provides a healthy existence for a small group of people, but it produces nothing but a small quantity of venison for which there is no demand. It causes money to change hands — a pack of cards can do that. I doubt if it could be said of a single deer forest, however barren and remote, that it could serve no better purpose". Plain speaking by a wealthy owner.

I have been painfully aware of the blood-sports racket all my life. It hit me direct and hard when I was eight years old. Our home was then on the Castle Lachlan Estate, Loch Fyne, where my father was an estate worker. Our near neighbour was Archie Crawford, blacksmith and crofter and a good man. His son Archie was ages with me and we were inseparable pals. Then one day a blow fell — which has had a searing affect on me for eighty years: Archie's father was charged by his closest neighbour, the head game-keeper Donald MacMillan, with having a pheasant in one of his rabbit snares. The landowner, John MacLachlan of MacLachlan, a lawyer with an Edinburgh firm, acted quickly and firmly. I suppose a short time would have been allowed for the family's removal, but at this late date it feels as if there were a moonlight flit. I never saw Archie again, and now won't.

This, of course, could not have happened today — or could it?

The 'Scotsman' newspaper of 21/4/77 reports the case of a farm manager on the Sutherland 60,000 acre estate belonging to Lt. Col. Moncrieff, being sacked on the spot. The Colonel defended his decision to order the instant dismissal of Mr MacDonald after he had learned that his 12-year-old son had been caught poaching on estate land.

To return to the Castle Lachlan pheasants — these birds were a continual menace to my father and his neighbour. Every year flocks of them were released in August, after having been hand-reared, into woodlands adjoining our crofts, and they quite literally devoured our potato crop. Potatoes were always lifted very early to avoid complete disappearance.

I have mentioned elsewhere a few of my later experiences of game and here is another.

Just this year I was advising a local estate-owner and supervising the planting of a small area with trees to be grown commercially. The cost of fencing against game encouraged by this owner's larger neighbours was just over £100 for each acre — before a single tree was planted. Existing fences were adequate for ordinary stock.

The deer population is obviously increasing. Motorists in this area have to be very wary on winter nights and several accidents have occurred. Last autumn four roe-deer took to jumping our garden fence and pinching our apples. There was a good crop, and the odd one was not missed, but when they moved in, in winter, and started browsing the trees I had to raise the fence to six feet, and now I find these trees have suffered a lot.

Hand-reared pheasants from a nearby estate have twice eaten about £5 worth of tulip species in my rock garden. We look on it as a rather grim joke. I objected much more to finding four shot jays, quite warm, hanging from the fence in the Scots pine plantation near my house. They are game-keepers' enemies. A neighbouring estate (Meiklour — Landsdowne) hand-rears, annually, over three thousand pheasants and this is happening on almost every estate and many farms all over Scotland. The game racket affects every acre of Scotland. We have a huge game population — not including the little (and big) fishes.

The Red Deer Commission admits that we now have around 300,000 of these large beasts roaming over our two North Regions with some also in Kirkcudbright. I estimate we have another 700,000 or so deer of several species, 7 million hares (white and brown), 15 million rabbits, 8 million pheasants, 5 million grouse and black game (pigeons, ducks, geese etc. I do not include here). This gives a rough total of 35 to 40 million animals and birds wandering over and living off the land — all to satisfy the sadistic anti-social blood-sportsman.

The killing of predators by game-keepers upsets the balance of

111

nature seriously. We have all seen the sad corpses hanging on their gibbets. I have seen noble birds, owls, buzzards and herons caught in gin-traps, some alive, some long dead and still in the trap. Perhaps the most disgusting evidence of the game-keeper's 'efficiency' I ever came across was on a nearby estate where over 50 hedgehogs were strung on a fence with other creatures great and small. It was a hot July day and the wood was reeking.

The toll in money taken from farming and forestry by the 35 to 40 million play-things of the sportsmen must be colossal yet we are constantly reminded that game is a 'money-spinning' industry, and that for one thing alone our rates benefit greatly from game.

I have estimated, from Perthshire's Valuation Roll, that the amount paid in 1973 in rates (agricultural land is de-rated and rates are based on the game on each estate) was £50,000. This would lead us to expect that for the *whole* of Scotland the rates paid would be £600,000 — for 19 million acres — not exactly a money-spinner for the country in rates.

Who benefits and who loses? The owner enjoys his fun and prestige and possibly lets the shoot, and collects the 'bag' of game. The tenant farmer or crofter — or state forester — has to put up high fencing or/and suffer the marauding millions.

We wonder about sacred cows in India.

The Highlands And Islands Development Board

I want to comment briefly here on the work of this board.

Its formation in 1965 by Willie Ross was considered by Michael Noble (now Lord Glenkinglass), then M.P. for Argyll, ex-Secretary of State for Scotland, as a lead-in to communism. In its ten years of existence under the two chairmen, Professor Grieve and Sir Andrew Gilchrist, there has been no approach to any socialist ideas.

Professor Grieve in his "Challenge" in the first annual report ends with the following two sentences indicating the kind of future he planned for the nine million acres in his charge: "Moreover, the vast bulk of the Highlands would remain visually as people know it except, simply, that there will be many more trees in its glens and moors, and more people either living in it or moving through it as visitors. And the Board is taking every step it humanly can to see that the bigger centres would be such that the country *would be proud of them.*" Could you beat it?

At the end of his stint, Sir Andrew Gilchrist bemoaned the fact that neither he nor Professor Grieve had done anything to solve the land problem. This is borne out by Prophet Smith, the extremely capable full-time member of the Board under both chairmen, with charge of land, in his article on land, entitled "Full Ahead", in the H.I.D.B.'s twenty-third issue of "North 7" from which I quote: "Where it (H.I.D.B.) has failed is in carrying through the recommendations of land surveys in the Strath of Kildonan and the Island of Mull. In both cases the crunch is that, as the Board's powers stand, these recommendations could only be given effect by the owners of the land, as the Board, despite views to the contrary, do not have legal powers of sanction on rural land questions. Furthermore, our very good relations with farmers and the National Farmers Union have not induced the landowners and the Scottish Landowners' Federation to advise members to give effect to our land proposals in the instances referred to. I hope that Parliament will in future make "siccar" what Parliament in 1965 failed to realise — that special procedures are required to compulsorily purchase rural land for the purpose of agricultural and forestry development. With such powers, not to be used recklessly, the Board could begin to effectively plan land development using land capability studies as the basis of its proposals and action."

When Professor Ken Alexander was appointed chairman in 1976 *The Times* must have sensed that something different would now happen in the Highlands. An article appeared (29th March 1976) by the reporter David Leigh from Inverness, with the spectacular heading "SPECTRE OF PUBLIC OWNERSHIP HAUNTING THE GROUSE MOORS". In it he gives the names and acreages of land owned by seven landlords, one of whom, the Duke of Atholl (130,000 acres) was not within the Crofting Counties. The other six were the Sutherland family, the Wills family, Vestey, Whitbread, Lovat and Burton — owning between them over 600,000 acres. Owners and acreages were taken from the recently published "Red Paper on Scotland" edited by Gordon Brown, the student-rector of Edinburgh University. *The Times,* significantly, did not acknowledge the source of information.

Thereafter David Leigh went on: "The Board's compulsory powers have never been used. . . . Professor Alexander who took up office only six weeks ago says that the situation (in the Highlands) had not changed a great deal in the Board's ten years of life, and continues: 'land is the major resource in the Highlands, and vast tracts of it may be capable of uses which will generate income and employment'. When a suitable case came up for compulsory purchase he would regard it as the Board's duty to take that course."

Ken Alexander is now in the middle of it and is certainly taking action, which, it is hoped, will result in rehabilitation of those nine million acres under his control. We do not want, anywhere in Scotland those "wildnernesses" much coveted by blood sportsmen and cranky conservationists.

We demand change — reclamation of land on a big scale and the return of men, women and children.

Prescription

When I started my investigations I hoped it would be possible to have the following treatment applied within twenty years by a Socialist U.K. Government. The present unrest in Scotland makes it likely that it will take at least fifty years, so I cannot hope to live to see any improvement. Having come so far, however, I shall proceed with my prescription.

As the Department of Geography, University of Glasgow, put it in their written 'Witness' to the Government, 'Land and Resource Use Survey 1972': "There should be a standardised land register . . . so that the ownership *and the geographical location* of all land holdings could be quickly established and changes in *ownership* and *use* be immediately recorded". As a follow-up to this land register it is recommended: "That a national Land Resource Registry be established with responsibility to undertake periodic land censuses".

This is exactly what many of us have been pressing for for years, and once the necessary Bill gets through Parliament, the job should not be expensive. The first census of agricultural land might take up to two years, but thereafter updating it would be easy. At the same time we must carry out a quick, perhaps rough and ready, but reliable assessment of the capability of all our land areas. I have a suspicion that our Scottish Department of Agriculture Fisheries and Food (DAFS), men with a deep knowledge of land and agriculture, could produce a useful capibility study with a minimum of field work. The Forestry Commission, the Hill Farm Research Organisation, the Macaulay Institute, the three agricultural colleges and the Nature Conservancy Council could pool the information they also already have and make it available for this purpose.

These three measures, land register, census of agriculture and forestry, and a simple capability study cover the first stage in the progressive improvement of land husbandry.

The second or mid-stage would be more drastic, and would affect all land whether privately or state owned. This would be the setting-up of a Land Commission. At the present time landlords can do as they please with land, and Government Departments — Agriculture, Forestry, Nature Conservancy and Defence — are constantly scrapping with each other on this matter. The multiple use of land is desirable, but with priority for agriculture and forestry. Determining how land should be allocated would be a matter of Government policy.

The objective would be to make sure that every acre in agriculture and forestry is fully productive, and we certainly have the highly skilled men in both industries, to guide the Commission as to what exactly is required to improve our short fall in husbandry, and furthermore, see to it that any decision and instructions to private estates are fully implemented. This will mean an immediate confrontation with the landlords, but it will also mean that at long last they will begin to realise that their power is waning, and it will acclimatise them to the fact that, in the not-too-distant future, their strong-hold will be broken.

Very big blunders can and will be made until we have this overseeing Commission. I will not elaborate on its composition, work-load etc., though I did work in the Forestry Department in Eire for over two years with a Land Commission and found it first class. There was nothing dogmatic on the part of the Commission: consultation with land users went on all the time, but the Land Commission had the final say.

As a result of these suggested changes much improvement could take place in ten years or so — better drainage, the disappearance of bracken and so on. Private land owners can be expected to resist the necessary legislation, but not too fiercely. However when it comes to administering my final prescription, the nationalisation of all land, the fun will begin.

We all in the Labour Party realise the terrific power there is within the body of landlords in Scotland — combined as they are in their trade union (one of the strongest in the world), The Scottish Landowners Federation. This is backed up by the almost equally powerful Scottish National Farmers Union (as a contrast, think of the 41,000 farm workers who have a union membership of only 4,300). Are we afraid to face the big boys? Perhaps we should be. After the publication of 'Acreocracy' in 1971, an article appeared in the journal of the S.L.F. written by a Perthshire bonnet laird, appealing to other landlords to enlist to "man the barricades in 1985". Lochdochart must be relieved to know that the crunch cannot now be expected so soon: it must however come some day, and the elimination of privileges — feudal superiority and the rest — will be accomplished through the ballot box.

Scottish landlords are possibly capable of handling our separatist tartan crowd, but they are scared stiff of a Socialist British Labour Party, and they have every reason to be. Nothing can or will stop us, not even the thousands of pounds[1] poured each year into the funds of reactionary political parties through Aims of Industry, British United Industrialists, the Economic League, Common Cause and so on. The barricades I thought would be a good ending, but now I think it a bit gloomy.

I shall tell one more story.

I have spoken to a duke only once in my lifetime — with an interesting result. In 1961 I was, surprisingly, appointed President of the Royal Scottish Forestry Society. The Forestry Commission had a show of equipment at the Bush near Edinburgh during my term of office, and on its opening day I was invited to lunch at the top table. All the top brass in forestry were there. I was placed opposite Chief Constable Merrilees and further down the table was the Duke of Buccleuch. Most of my talk was with the Chief, but, at one stage, the Duke, an ex-President, leant over and congratulated me on being President, and we spoke for a few minutes. Then Chief Merrilees whispered "Who was that you were talking to?" and, on being told, was obviously impressed. When, later, I complained to him about the desperate difficulty I had had coming from 'the ferry' to the Bush (this was before the Forth Road Bridge was opened) he offered to help me on my return trip. I was led back to Queensferry by a police car with its light flashing, to find the ferry waiting to leave, having been warned that the customer arriving was to be 'last on — first off'. (I understand they were expecting a criminal in handcuffs).

---

(1) A special pamphlet from the Labour Research Department in 1974 declared the subscribed figure for that year to be £1,000,000. In their monthly magazine one year later (1975) this had increased to £1,600,000. The figure for 1976 is not reported to have gone up but is still a very considerable £1,218,000.

A ROYAL COMMISSION ON LAND
COVERING GREAT BRITAIN

We have had over the past 100 years or so plenty of enquires into land in all its aspects. We need one more. A Royal Commission appointed to enquire deeply into the failure of private landlords in their so-called stewardship of land in *Britain*. The Commission to be composed of men and women from all classes of society. To be given strong, clear, specific terms of reference, and a reasonable time, say three years, in which to report back, again with clear conclusions and recommendations. These recommendations to be implemented as soon as reasonably possible. Only a Labour Government can do this and the sooner the better.

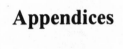

Appendices

Appendix 1

SHETLAND AND ORKNEY

Note: The figures which follow for Orkney and Shetland are for 1874. These areas were not mapped by Millman.

SHETLAND

Land area:	352,337 acres
Inland water:	9,631 acres

Private Estates from 30,000 acres to 10,000 acres

Owner	Estate	Acre
Busta Est. Tr.	Busta House	29,820
Bruce, Tutors and Curators of Wm Arthur	Symbister	25,180
Lady Nicolson of Nicolson	Cheltenham	24,785
Maj. J. M. Cameron of Garth	Annsbrae	24,363
A. J. Griersun	Quendale House	22,006
Mrs B. G. H. Robertson	(Lerwick)	13,700
Earl of Zetland	(London)	13,600
Lunn Ests. Tr.	Sand Lodge, Sandwick	13,330
R. T. C. Scott	Melby House	13,020
Elizabeth Bruce	Sand Lodge	12,338
J. Leask	Sound	11,847
G. H. B. Hay	Hayfield House	11,105

Total of Estates down to 10,000 acres

12 Estates — 215,094

Summary

12 estates down to 10,000	215,094 acres
20 estates 10,000 to 1,000 acres	55,400 acres

Total of Estates down to 1,000 acres

32 Estates — 270,494 acres

Total area of county .... 352,337 acres

Total area of private Estates down to 1,000 acres .... 270,494 acres

ORKNEY

Land area:	240,848 acres
Inland water:	8,563 acres

Private Estates from 60,000 acres to 10,000 acres

Owner	Estate	Acres
J. G. M. Heddle	Melsetter House	50,410
Earl of Zetland (London)	Zetland Ests.	29,846
David Balfour	Balfour Castle	29,054

Total of Estates down to 10,000 acres

3 estates — 109,310

Summary

3 estates 60,000 to 10,000 acres	109,310 acres
8 estates 10,000 to 5,000 acres	50,600 acres
11 estates 5,000 to 1,000 acres	22,100 acres

Total of Estates down to 1,000 acres
22 estates — 182,000 acres

Total area of county .... 240,848 acres

Total area of private Estates down to 1,000 acres .... 182,000 acres

I hope these lists of ownerships in these two islands for 1874 will interest readers including Shetlanders and Orcadians. It is a pity that Dr. Millman did not manage to do his work on these, but it should not be very difficult for the folks of both islands to do a quick, cheap survey of present ownership and have their boundaries placed on one-inch maps and have acreages worked out by planimeter. If the interest is taken up on this matter and help is required I shall be only too glad to assist.

Appendix 2

THE SCOTTISH OFFICE (1970s) AND A LAND REGISTER

The question of a follow-up on the Land Register of 1874 has been mooted for a long time but came to a head on 19th February 1976 in the First Scottish Standing Committee dealing with the Crofting (Scotland) Bill when a resolution asking for a Land Register for the crofting area was put forward. The climax came in the reply of the Under Secretary of State, Mr Hugh Brown, responsible for land, and I quote: "Although I may be accused, if not by my Hon. Friend then by some of my other Hon. Friends outside, of trying to convert pragmatism into a new philosophy, I must confess that, having been in Caithness and Sutherland a few months ago, and having come down the Strath of Kildonan on a lovely evening — travelling with British Rail at such a leisurely rate one has time to admire the scenery — I thought 'What the hell would we want to do with these acres of land in any case?'"

I hope my friend (we sat together for a whole day at the Party (Labour) Conference in Perth in 1971) will take in the spirit in which it is meant this message: Dear Hugh, please do not worry yourself. Go, get that land for us. We shall advise you exactly what to do with it and, furthermore, see to it that it is done. Yours, John and many others."

As a postscript to that message it should be noted that the *Daily Telegraph* colour magazine for 18 April 1975 had an article on Suisdale estate (17,000 acres) in this strath, now belonging to a young financier named Edward Reeves and reputedly costing him £1,600,000 (£1,000 per acrè). It was bought for its peace, its sporting value — fishing and shooting. Developing it for its actual, natural use — agriculture — was never mentioned. I gather the Forestry Commission were out to purchase but could not face this outrageous price. Reeves was a director of Reunion Properties, speculators, which sold out to Jardine Matheson's for a multi-million profit in 1973 (at a share price so inflated it nearly wrecked the Hong Kong stock market, where Jardine Mathesons raised the money). Have not the Government through the Scottish Office the power to force good husbandry on such valuable land as there is in this strath or take it over and have it developed at the owner's expense? What about it Hugh?

Appendix 3

HANSARD OF 13 JUNE 1977
Written Answers on Community Land Prices

Mr Welsh asked the Secretary of State for Scotland what has been the amount of land purchased in Scotland under the provisions of the Community Land Act, the purposes for which this land is to be used and the cost involved, region by region and nationally.

Mr McElhone: Following is the infomation:

Community Land Scheme: Position at 31st March 1977

Region	Industry £	acres	Commerce £	acres	Total	acres
Central	16,500	5.90	—	—	16,500	5.90
Dumfries and Galloway	27,000	15.50	—	—	27,000	15.50
Fife	20,400	18.48	—	—	20,400	18.48
Grampian	43,500	10.51	22,750	0.14	66,250	10.65
Lothian	137,882	15.01	—	--	137,882	15.01
Strathclyde	—	—	159,00	1.00	159,000	1.00
Total	245,282	65.40	181,750	1.14	427,032	6.54

Notes:

1. Provisional figures subject to revision when Community Land accounts for 1976-77 are submitted.

2. Figures exclude staff and administration costs and interest charges.

Author's note: It is illuminating to break these prices paid down into cost per acre. These are approximately as follows:

Central £2,796

Dumfries and Galloway £1,941

Fife £1,104

Grampian £6,221

Lothian.................... £9,186

Strathclyde................. £159,000

Appendix 4

PUBLIC OWNERSHIP OF LAND
Development priority - Nationalisation

In *"Labour's Programme 1973"* we recognised that the priority for action on land should be land required for development. Legislation has already been passed to cope with this. In the meantime, the NEC has published proposals *("The Public Ownership of Agricultural Land -Immediate Proposals for Action")* for the creation of a public stake in agricultural land through the voluntary transfer of ownership of agricultural land as a means of paying capital transfer tax and the proposed wealth tax. Provision would also be made for

123

the voluntary sale of land to the state, regardless of tax considerations. This would not mean that there would be state farming; the state would be the landlord, with the land let out to tenant farmers. This interim measure, however, is not intended in any way to detract from the basic policy of the Party: that is, the public ownership of all land - and especially the abolition of the large-scale private ownership of land: Under this interim scheme, publicly owned agricultural land would be vested in an Agricultural Land Commission.

Labour's Programme for Britain 1976

Appendix 5

LAND NATIONALISATION
At the Labour Party 1972 Annual Conference in Inverness

This Conference, following the previous year's in Perth when "Acreocracy" was on the Party bookstall, must have had a stirring-up on land nationalisation amongst the constituencies as four of them put forward resolutions pressing for full-blooded nationalisation of all land in Scotland.

This ended in the Executive accepting an agreed resolution asking for the setting-up of a Working Party to go deeply into this question of nationalisation and to report back to the 1973 Conference. The resolution was proposed by Sandy Lindsay (now, sadly a high-up resolute SNP) for Inverness, and seconded by myself for Perth and E. Perthshire. It was unanimously passed by the delegates.

An interim report was forwarded in time for 1973 Conference. The executive must have taken cold feet. It was not discussed on the floor of the Conference and nothing has been heard of it since. Should not, even at this late date, the present (1977) executive of the Scottish Council let us know what happened and where we go from here?

Appendix 6

HANSARD OF 6 NOVEMBER 1963
Report of debate in House of Commons on Housing and Land

Mr William Ross (Kilmarnock) speaking: My right hon. Friend the member for Fulham (Mr Michael Stewart) said that there was a time when the Crown owned all the land. Theoretically, in Scotland, it still does. We will have a Bill about land tenure in Scotland. I have often thought that, if we resurrected the rights of the Crown — there is not a loyal Tory Member who would object to that, surely — we would nationalise the land in Scotland in a one-clause Bill.

Appendix 7

HIGHLANDS CHANGES ADVOCATED

No-one with direct experience of the Highlands can avoid feeling uneasy about land use.

That was the view of Sir Andrew Gilchrist, former chairman of the Highlands and Islands Development Board, when he told the Scotia Agricultural Club in Edinburgh:

"The nineteenth century saw half the Highlanders being made into gillies and trained to take tips, while the other half, to stop them going to America, were bribed to stay on the land as crofters.

"The surprising thing is how far this nineteenth-century system is still a continuing influence on the Highland way of life today".

A full answer to the problem, by development and diversification, had still to be worked out, but he said, but *(sic)* some curtailment of the "empire of grouse and deer" was needed.

He backed present HIDB policy, under the chairmanship of Professor Alexander, to get more say in land use, and pointed out that at least 500,000 Highland acres could contribute much more meat if better managed.

Paradoxically, he defended Highland landowners against the accusation that their estates were too large and that they made undue profits from blood sports.

For example, he said, if the Prime Minister wanted to contribute as many tons of meat equivalent from typical land in the Highlands as he does from his 200 acres in the Home Counties, he would need 12,300 acres to do so, and have to accept the "execration and obloquy" that goes with being a Highland landlord.

As for blood sports, there were only 200,000 grouse in the Highlands, with about 40,000 shot each year, a trivial amount of money to divide among a few hundred landowners.

He felt the significance of recent efforts in the Highlands and Islands was that loss of the British empire had forced colonisation of our own country, and it was proving successful.

Professor Donald Mackay, editor of a recent book on the economics of devolution and independence, emphasised the importance of investing surplus oil revenue in long-term projects. . .

Farming, fishing and forestry would obviously be candidates for heavy investment, along with steel, shipbuilding and railways; there are many opportunities.

"Your aim is not immediate profits, but an efficient industry in ten or 20 years time, and as far as farming is concerned, you are better judges than I am".

The Scotsman 1st June 1977

Appendix 8
RUSKICH

The other farm we visited, in Glenlyon, was in fact a small holding belonging to the Forestry Commission, consisting of just over 30 acres of grass and 40 acres of outrun. It was farmed, in his spare time, by Mr J. Campbell-Smith who is the resident Forestry Commission foreman in that area. On his 30 acres, Mr Campbell-Smith carries 43 breeding cows and calves and a bull. This works out at approximately 0.6 of an acre per cow and calf. In addition, the silage requirement for the cattle during the winter is cut from the 30 acres of grass. Mr Campbell-Smith is not only an enthusiastic student of Voisin who is a leading authority on grassland management, but is also an extremely successful exponent of his system. A lot of people didn't really quite believe their eyes particularly as the farm is approximately 750 ft high with a rainfall of around 80″ and a winter which appears to last for about 7 months.

Tremendous interest was shown in this farm and indeed it was probably the most interesting item with which we dealt on this Course. A number of people expressed their desire to come back and see it under more restful climatic conditions. One of the parties which visited it in the morning were involved in a cloudburst and a number of people got extremely wet.

Scottish Landowner Jan. 1967 No. 126

Appendix 9
GAME-BIRD DAMAGE TO YOUNG CONIFER PLANTATIONS

The usual and accepted damage by four-footed animals is very well known. It is very different with our feathered enemies, particularly grouse, who are not supposed to do any harm to young conifers. It has, however, been conclusively proved that anything up to 2,000 pine buds have been counted in the crops of birds. . In the case of capercailzie a recent count of 10,000 Sitka spruce buds was made in the crop of one bird. Serious damage follows, the trees remaining deformed for many years, and I have even some Scots pine which never did recover.

Appendix 10

· I am very fortunate to own the 1874 Doomsday Book for Scotland.

If any readers can put me on to the following Government publications, I shall be very grateful:

—Full Report of Highland and Island Commission 1883 (Napier Report)
—The Royal Commission (Highlands and Islands 1892). Complete written matter and maps (Red Deer Report) or maps only
—Final Report of the Forestry Sub-Committee of the Reconstruction Committee (Cd. 8881) 1918 (The Acland Report)
—Report of the Departmental Committee on Deer Forests 1919 (Chairman: Sir John Stirling-Maxwell).

Appendix 11

In conclusion, we assert that the land of Scotland is the natural inheritance of the people of Scotland. Private ownership of land is a medieval concept, designed to ensure the dominance of a self-perpetuating oligarchy. It is an affront to reason for a private individual to claim ownership of mountains, lochs and rivers. This first Report — if implemented by the next Labour Government — would go far to redress the balance in favour of the people.

Scottish Council of the Labour Party
Executive Committee Working Party 1972

INDEX

Only references from the text and notes to the Counties are included in this index. Tables of Estates and owners, graphs and statistics are not included.

Abercairney (Estate) 53
Abercromby, *Lord* 60
Aberdeen (County) 47-49
Aberdeen University 14, 92
Abington House (Estate) 72
Absentee Landlordism 24
Acland, F. D. 94
Acland Report 94
'The Acreocracy of Perth-
shire; Who owns our
land' 13, 14, 116
Agricultural College,
Edinburgh 10
Agricultural Colleges
(Scotland) 10, 98, 107, 115
— : Advisors 104
Agricultural Economic Deve-
lopment Council (Little
Nedy) 108, 109
'Agricultural Statistics 1975'
104
Agriculture 7, 104-109, 126
See also Agriculture:
private Estates *Various
headings under* Land
Agriculture, Fisheries and
Food, Department of
(also Ministry of) 34, 95,
100, 106, 115, 116
'Agriculture into the 1980s'
108, 109
Agriculture: private estates 7,
54,104-109
See also Land: private
estates
Agriculture: private estates:
Highlands 24, 104, 107,
125, 126
Agriculture: productivity. *See
also* productivity: land
Agriculture Training Board
108
Ailsa, *Marquis of* 77
Aims of Industry 117
Airlie, *Earl of* 51
Airthry Castle (Estate) 60

Alcohol Manufacturers: land
interests 27, 27, 34, 53,
54, 84
Alexander, *Professor* Ken
114, 114, 125
Alice Holt (Research Station)
96
Altonside Distributing Nur-
sery 11
Altyre (Estate) 10, 43, 43
Anderson, Mark L. 96, 98
Angus (County) 51-52
Animals, Farm: condition of
stock 108
Anstruther (Family) of
Balcaskie 22, 63
— of Balcaskie, *Sir* R. H.
22, 63
Applecross (Estate) 27
Arbuthnot (EState) 49
Arbuthnot, *Lord* 49-50
Ardgowan (Estate) 70
Ardross (Estate) 26
Argyll (County) 33-37
Argyll, *Duke of* 33, 34, 34, 64
See also Campbell
(Family)
Armadale (Estate) 30
Arniston (Estate) 63
Arrisdale (Estate) 54
Asquith, H. H. (Prime
minister) 94
Atholl (Estate) 53, 93
Atholl, *Duke of* 48, 53, 53, 90
114
Atholl Highlanders 90
Ayr (County) 77-79
B.B.C. *See* British Broadcasting
poration
B.O.T. *See* Board of Trade
Bachnagairn (Estate) 51
Baillie (Family) 27,30
See also Burton, *Lord*
Baird Coal Co. 77
Balbirnie (Estate) 62
Balfour (Family) 27, 62, 69

— *Mr & Mrs* 24, 62
— *Mrs* 24,62
— A. J. 27,69
Balfour, Robert Wardlaw Ramsay 60
Balnanoth (Estate) 51
Banff (County) 45-47
Bannockburn 10
Barra 47
Bathgate (Estate) 66
Benbecula 47
Berbeth, Dalmellington (Estate) 77
Berwick (County) 75-77
Binning, *Lord* 68, 69
Bisset & Sons (Blairgowrie) Ltd 104
Blair Castle 90
Blood Sports
See also: Blood
See also Game
Board of Trade 11, 92
Booze *See* Alcohol manufacturers: land interests
Bosville-Macdonald of Sleat, *Lord*. *See* Macdonald of Armadale, *Lord*
Botanic Garden, Royal (Edinburgh) 10
Brasher, Chris 90
Breadalbane (Estate) 52, 106
Breadalbane, *Earl of* 33, 52, 53
See also Campbell (Family)
Brechin Castle (Estate) 51
British Association for the Advancement of Science: Annual Meeting, Dundee 1968 91
British Broadcasting Corporation 90-91
British United Industrialists 117
Brodick Castle (Estate) 37
Brodie (Family) of Lethen 42
Brown , Gordon 15, 107, 114
Brown, Hugh (Under Secretary of State for Scotland) 122
Bryden, John 105
Buccleuch, *Duke of* 7, 47, 67, 71, 72, 74, 80, 83, 90, 117
Buchanan, Macdonald—, A. J. 27

Burleigh, *Lord* 60
Burton, *Lord* 27, 30
See also Baillie (Family)
Bush Research Station 96, 117
Bute (County) 37-38
Bute, (Family) 63, 71
— *Marquis of* 37, 77, 79
Cabrach (Estate) 46
Caithness (County) 22-23
Calder, John 61
Callander (Estate) 82
Callander House (Estate) 65
Cally (Estate) 82
Cambusdoon (Estate) 77
Cameron (Family) of Lochiel 26, 30
Campbell (Family) 33-34, 42, 52-53, 53, 76
See also Argyll, *Duke of*
Breadalbane *Earl of*
Campbell, I. N.
Cawdor, *Earl of*
Mackie Campbell
Campbell, Gordon *(Lord Campbell of Croy)* (Secretary of State for Scotland) 34
Campbell, I. N. 34
Campbell-Smith, J. 126
Capital Transfer Tax 93, 123
Carnwath (Estate) 72
Castle Lachlan (Estate) 9, 110, 111
Castlemilk (Estate) 80
Cathcart, *Mrs* Jean Mac-Adam 77, 82
Cawdor, *Earl of* 42
See also Campbell (Family)
Cayzer, *Major* H. S. 46
Clackmannan (County) 60-61
'Challenge' 113
Clerk of Penicuik, *Sir* G. D. 67
Clyde, (River) 70
Coal: mining rights and rents 60, 62, 65, 66, 67, 69, 70, 71, 72, 77, 80, 82
Colquhoun (Family) of Luss 64
Comlongan (Estate) 80
Commissioners; Forestry Commission 95, 100

Common Cause 117
Community Land Act 122
Compulsory Land Acquisition
    See Land: Compulsory
    Acquisition
    Land: nationalisation
Conservative Government
    1959-64: relations with
    Forestry Commission 97
Conservative Government
    1970-74: relations with
    Forestry Commission 96
Countryside Commission,
    Scottish 24
Cowdray, *Viscount* 47-48, 49
Craigengillan (Estate) 82
Crathes (Estate) 49
Crawford, Archie 110
Crichton-Stewart (Family)
    See Bute (Family)
    Bute, *Marquis of*
Crofting Counties: composition of 37, 42
Crofting (Scotland) Bill 121
Crofting Commission 26
Cromarty (County)
    See Ross and Cromarty
    (County)
Crown ownership of land,
    theoretical 124-5
Cullen House 10, 45
Culmony (Estate) 42
Cumming, Gordon- (Family)
    43
Cunningham, *Dr* 34, 107
Currie, *Sir* Donald 9
'Daily Telegraph' 122
Dalhousie, *Earl of* 51
Dalmahoy (Estate) 62, 67
Dalmellington (Estate) 77
Deer 111, 111
Deer Forests 110
    *See also various entries
    under* Game
Deer, Red 27, 34, 100
    *See also various entries
    under* Game
    Sport, blood
    Forestry Commission:
    Game control
    'Red Deer Commission
    1895'
    Forestry: Deer Control

Deer, Red; Farming 34.35, 54
Department of —
    For Government Departments see under name of
    each department
Department of Geography,
    University of Glasgow
    115
De Walden, Howard, *Lord* 78
Dochfour (Estate) 30
Douglas Home, *Sir* Alex 76
    See also Home of the
    Hirsel, *Lord*
Drummond Castle (Estate)
    53, 105
Drummond Moray (Family)
    53
Duff, Gordon — *Major* 45
'The Dukes' 82
Dulverton, *Lord* 27
    see also Wills (Family)
Dumbarton (County) 64-65
Dumfries (County) 80-82
Dundas of Arniston (Family)
    See Zetland, *Earl of*
Dundas of Arniston, Robert
    See also Zetland, *Earl of*
Dunecht (Estate) 49
Dunsyre (Estate) 72
Duntreath Castle (Estate) 65
Dunvegan (Estate) 30
Dupplin (Estate) 53
Dunro (Estate) 49
Eagle Star Insurance Co. 44
Eaglesham (Estate) 70
East Lothian (County) 68-70
East of Scotland Agricultural
    College 98
Economic Forestry Group 80,
    91
    See also private forestry
    groups
Economic League 117
Edinburgh University 15
    — Professorship of Forestry 96, 98
Education: Forestry
    See Forestry Commission: Education
    Forestry Education
Eglinton, *Earl of* 77
Eire: Forestry Department 116
    See Forestry Department
    (Eire)

Eire: Land Commission 116
Elizabeth II, *Queen of U.K.*
    47, 51
Elizabeth, *Queen Mother* 51
Esk, South (Estate- 105
Estate Factors: private estates
    91
Estate Management: private
    estates 53, 74, 91-93
    See also under Estates,
    private
Estates, private
    *See*Agriculture: private
    estates
    Estate factors, private
    estates
    Estate management:
    private estates
    Eviction: private estates
    Forestry: private estates
    Game (various sub head-
    ings)
    Land: private estates
    Landlords: private
    estates
    Private Forestry Groups
    Sport, blood
Eviction: private estates 110
Factors 91
Fairburn (Estate) 90
Falkland (Estate) 63
Falkland Estate Trustees 63
Farm Livestock: condition of
    108
Farming *See*
    Agriculture
    Agriculture: private
    estates
    Land: private estates
Farquarson (Family) of
    Invercauld 47
Fassque House (Estate) 49
Fasifern (Estate) 27
Fencing: game control 27, 111
    See Game: fencing
Ferguson, Munro— (Family)
    See Munro-Ferguson
    (Family)
Fergusson of Kilkerran
    (Family) 77
Feudal superiority 75, 117,
    124-25
Fife (County) 62-64
Fife County Council 62

Fife, *Duke of* 44, 45, 47, 51
'56th Annual Forgstry Com-
    mission Report' 95
Findlay, Mr 46
'First Annual Forestry Com-
    mission Report' 93
First Scottish Standing Com-
    mittee 121
Fishing
    See various headings
    under Game, Sport,
    blood
Fleming (Family) of Dundee
    34
Forbes (Family) of Callander
    65
Forestry *See principally*
    Forestry Commission
    Forestry: private estates
Forestry Act 1919 94, 99
Forestry Commission 7, 11,
    34, 34, 45-46, 82, 93-
    100, 115, 116
    —Aberdeen Division 11
    —Acres owned 17, 34-35,
    82
    —Alice Holt Research
    Station 96
    —Altonside Distributing
    Nursery 11
    —Bush Research Station
    96, 117
    —census of private
    woodlands 92
    —commissioners 95, 100
    —education 97-99
    —First Annual Report
    93-94
    —56th Annual Report 95
    —Forestry Act 1919 94,
    99
    —Fort Augustus confer-
    ence 100
    —Game control 45-46,
    95, 99-100
    —grants 91, 92, 93, 99
    —Interim Forest Autho-
    rity 94
    —land prices 97,101-104,
    122
    —Monnaughty Forest
    11, 43,
    —planting programmes
    97, 99

—powers of 94, 99
—relations with Con-
servative Government
1970-74 96, 97
—relations with John
McEwen 45-6, 98, 99
—relations with private
landlords 45-6, 93
—reorganisation 1964 95
—research stations 96
—Speymouth Forest 11
—subsidies. *See* Forestry
Commission: grants
—Teindland Forest 11,
43, 45
—timber production
(projected) 99
—uniform 98
—wages 99
Forestry: deer control
See Game: fencing
Game: control
Forestry Department (Eire)
11, 96, 116
Forestry: Education 97-99
Forestry: fencing *See* Game:
fencing
Forestry Finance Groups
See Private Forestry
Groups
Forestry: game control 127
See also Gamez; control
Game: fencing
Forestry Commission: Game control
Forestry Groups, private
See Private Forestry
Groups
Forestry: planting pro-
grammes 92-3, 97
Forestry: pre Forestry Com-
mission 93-94
Forestry: private estates 7, 27,
49, 54, 90-3, 93-4
Forestry: productivity. *See*
productivity: land
Forestry: subsidies 95, 99
See also Forestry Com-
mission grants
Forestry: training 10, 97-101
Fort Augustus: Forestry
Commission Conference
100
Fort William 99
Forteviot, *Lord* 53

Fortingall (Estate) 9
Fothringham, Stuart—
(Family) 53
Fraser (Family)
See Lovat, *Lord*
'Full ahead' *Article in 'North
7'* 113
Galloway, *Earl of* 82
Game 7, 45, 54, 54, 56, 106,
110-2, 125, 127
See also Sport, blood
Game: control 45, 95, 99-100,
111
Game: deer forests 27
Game: fencing 27, 45, 111
Gamekeepers 111-112
Garden of Breadalbane 106
Garth Castle (Estate) 9
Geography, Department of,
Glasgow University 125
Gilchrist, *Sir* Andrew 113, 115
Gilmour, *Sir* John 62, 67
Gilmour (Family) of Lundin
62
Gladstone (Family) of Fasque
49
Gladstone, W. E. 49
Glamis (Estate) 51, 105
Glasgow: Parks Department
10
Glasgow University: Depart-
ment of Geography 115
Glenavon (Estate) 46
Gleneagles hotel 54
Glenforsa (Estate) 34
Glenkinglass, *Lord* 34, 113
Glenlyon, 54, 126
Gordon (Family) 47
Gordon, W. G. 54
Gordon Cumming (Family) 43
Gordon-Duff, Major 45
Gordon of Cluny, Colonel 47
Gordon, Richmond and,
Duke of 44, 45-6, 47
Grandtully (Estate) 53
Grants: agriculture 106
Grants; forestry
See Forestry Commission
grants
Grieve, *Professor* 113
Grouse 100, 106, 109, 125, 127
See also Game
Sport, blood
Gryfe, *Lord* Taylor of 95

Haddington, *Earl* of 68, 69, 76
Hamilton, *Duke* of 37, 66, 71, 72
Hares 111
    See also Game
    Sport, blood
Healey, Denis 91, 93
Heath, Edward 97, 100
    See also Conservative
    Government 1970-74
Hereward Wake, *Major* 31
Heriot-Watt University 10
'Highland Forum: 1968
    Report' 105
'Highland landlordism; article
    in "Red Paper on Scot-
    land"' 15
Highlands: agriculture
    See Agriculture: private
    estates: Highlands
Highlands: future of 113-4,
    125
Highlands and Islands Deve-
    lopment Board 34, 34,
    113-4, 125
Hill Farming Research
    Organisation 34, 107, 115
Hirsel, home of the, *Lord*
    See Home of the Hirsel,
    Lord
Home, Charles 53
Home Grown Timber Depart-
    ment 11
Home of the Hirsel, *Lord*
    70, 76, 83
Hong Kong Stock Market 122
Hopetoun (Estate) 66
Hopetoun, *Lord* 72
Howard de Walden, *Lord* 78
Huntley, *Marquis of* 47
Husbandry
    See Agriculture
Inchape, *Earl of* 51
Interim Forestry Authority 94
International Biometeoro-
    logical Congress 1975 105
Inveraray Castle 34
Invercauld (Estate) 47
Inverness (County) 29-33
Irish Forestry Department 11,
    96, 116
Janson, *Mrs*
    See Sutherland, Countess
    of

Jardine, Matheson 122
Jenkins, L. A. 95
Johnston, Tom 13
Jones, James, Timber
    merchants 10, 11
Keir (Estate) 70
Kellie, *Earl of* 60
Kerse House (Estate) 65
Kildonan, Strath of 113, 122
Kilmarnock Estates 78
Kincardine (County) 49-50
Kinnaird Castle (Estate) 51,
    105
Kinnoull, *earl of* 53
Kinross (County) 61-62
Kirkcudbright (County) 82-83
Knockespock (Estate) 47
Labour Government 115, 117,
    118
    —1964-70 92, 97
    —1974- 97
Labour Party 123, 127
Labour Party Conference,
    Perth 1971 122
    Inverness 1972 124
Labour Party Research
    Department 117 (note)
'Land and Resource use Survey
    1972' 115
Land capability studies 114,
    115
Land censuses 115
Land Commission 116, 116,
    118, 124
Land: compulsory purchase 95, 99, 114
Land: crown ownership, of, theoretical
    124-5
Land: management
    See Land: private estates
Land: nationalisation 7, 96, 114, 116,
    123-4, 124-5, 127
Land: prices 97, 101-4, 122
Land: private estates 54, 74, 90-93, 109.
Land productivity
    See productivity: land
Land reclamation 107
Land register 7, 15, 78, 115, 121-1
Land register 1874 8, 15
land resource registry 115
Land, Royal Commission on: desir-
    ability of 118
Land speculation 97, 101
Land use
    See land: private estates

133

Landlordism, absentee 24
Landlords: privates estates 7, 13, 14,
    63, 90-93, 105, 110-11, 113, 115,
    116, 17
    See also Land: private estates
Landlords: private estates: aid for 90-
    93, 106-7
    —domination of Forestry Com-
    mission chairmanship 95
    —grants 90-93
    —Perthshire 13-14
Landowners, Federation of, Scottish
    113, 116
Landownership: Perthshire 13-14
'Lands and Heritages 1874' 8, 15
Lanfine (Estate) 77
Landsdowne, *Marquis of* 93, 111
Lauder (Estate) 75
Lauderdale, *Lord* 76
Lawson, Edwin 104
Ledlanet (Estate) 61
Lee and Carnwath (Estate) 72
Leigh, David 144
Leith Harbour·67
Leven and Melville, *Earl of* 42
Lewis (Isle of) 26
Lindsay, Sandy 124
Lining out machine 96
Linlithgow, *Lord* 72
Little Neddy 108, 109
Livestock: condition 108
Lobster farming 69
Lochdochart 117
Lochfyneside 9, 99
Lochiel (Estate) 26, 30
Lockhart, S. F. MacDonald— 72
Logan Estates 79
'Lord of the Isles' 70
Lothian, *Marquis of* 67, 84
Lovat, *Lord* 30, 31, 93, 98, 100
Lude (Estate) 54
Lundin (Estate) 62
Luttrell, Mr. *See* Munro-Ferguson
    (Family)
Lyon, River 9
Macaulay Institute 115
MacCallum of Muckairn 31
MacDonald, *Mr* 110
MacDonald of Sleat, *Lord. See*
    MacDonald of Armadale, *Lord*
MacDonald of Armadale, *Lord* 30
MacDonald-Buchanan, A. J. 27
MacDonald-Lockhart, S. F.
McEwen, John 9-12,43-4, 45-6, 62-3,
    98-9

McEwen, *Sir* John 76
McGrath, John 50, 125
Mackay, Donald 50, 125
Mackenzie (Family) of Ross 26
Mackie, John 95, 99
Mackie Campbell 33
    See also Campbell (Family)
MacLachlan of MacLachlan, John 110
MacLean, Charles Ogilvy, *Capt* 51
MacLennan, David 24
MacLennan, R., *M.P.* 24
MacLeod of MacLeod (Family) 30
MacMillan, Donald 110
'The making of the crofting Com-
    munties' 47
Mansfield, *Earl of* 53, 60, 80-90, 93
Maps
    See Millman, *Dr* Roger: Maps
Marchmont (Estate) 76
Masserene (Family) of Mull 34
'Masters, Brian "The Dukes"' 82
Matheson (Family) 23, 26
Matheson, Jardine— 122
Maxwell (Family) of Monreith 79
Maxwell, *Sir* John Stirling 110
Maxwell, *Sir* William 70
Meggernie (Estate) 54, 93
Meikleour (Estate) 111
Melville, Leven &, *Earl of* 42
Menzies (Family) of Perthsire 53, 53
Merilees, Chief Constable 117
Middleton, *Lord* 27
Midlothian (County) 67-8
Millan, Bruce *Secretary of State for
    Scotland* 7
Miller, Margaret 12
Millman, *Dr* Roger 14
    —maps 7, 8, 14-15, 70, 75, 76, 77,
    82, 121
'Minard Castle' 70
Ministry of —
    For Government ministries see
    under name of each ministry
Monnaughty Forest 11, 43
Moncrieff, *Lt. Col.* 110
Monreith (Estate) 79
Montrave (Estate) 62
Montrose, *Duke of* 53, 65
Moray (County) 43-45
Moray, Drumond— (Family) 53
Moray, *Earl of* 43, 53, 62
Morrison (Family) of Islay 34
Morton, *Earl of* 67
Mull (Isle of) 113

Munro-Ferguson (Family) 27, 62-63
—A.B.L. 27, 62-63
Murray (Family) 48, 53. *See also*
  Atholl, *Duke of*
  Mansfield, *Earl of*
Murray, *Sir* J. of Philipshaugh &
  Melgund 74
Murthly (Estate) 53, 93
Nairn (County) 42-43
Napier, *Lord* 26, 74
'Napier Report 1885' 26
National Farmers Union 113, 116
Nationalisation: land
  See land: nationalisation
Nationalised industries 96, 97
Nature Conservancy Council 115, 116
Noble (Family) 34, 34
Noble, Michael 34, 113
Norfolk, *Duke of* 80, 82
North of Scotland Hydro Electric
  Board 30
'North 7' 113
Novar (Estate) 27
Obilvy (Family) 51, 51
Ogilvy, David 51
Openshaw, Keith 14
Ordnance Survey 14
Ordnance Survey 7, 14
Orkney 15, 63, 120-1
Orr, *Sir* Andrew 60
'Our Scottish Noble Families' 13
Pan-bound soils 96
Peebles (County) 73-74
Penninghame (Estate) 79
Perth & Kinross Fabian Society 13-14
Perth (County) 52-56, 106, 107, 126
Perthshire Valuation Roll 111
Pests 108, 11
  See also Game
Pheasants 111, 111
  See also Game
  Sport, blood
Philliphaugh (Estate) 74
Plant lining out machine 96
Poaching 45-6, 110
Policies 51-105
Polkennet (Estate) 66
Pollok and Keir (Estate) 70
Pollockshields U. F. Church Mission
  10
Portland, *Duke of* 22, 77
Private Forestry Groups 72, 74, 80, 80,
  81, 82, 84, 91, 93
  See also Forestry: private estates

Productivity: land 92, 94, 97, 99, 104-5,
  105-6, 107, 108, 112, 114, 116, 122
"Public ownership of agriculture:
  Immediate proposals for action"
  123, 125, 126
Pulp Mills, 99,
Pyatt, D. G. 96
Quarrying: rents 70
Queen Elizabeth II 47, 51
Queen Mother 51
Queen Victoria 47
Rabbits 111
  See also Game
  Sport, blood
Raehills (Estate) 80
Raith (Estate) 27
Ramsay, Robert Balfour Wardlaw 60
Rankin, K. N. 91, 92
Rannoch (Estate) 54
Reconstruction Committee of Cabinet
  1916 94
Record Office, Edinburgh 14
Red deer
  See deer, red
'Red Deer Commission 1895' 30-31
Red Deer Commission 111
'Red Paper on Scotland' 15, 107, 114
Reeves, Edward 122
Register House, Edinburgh 14, 15
Renfrew (County) 70-71
Reunion Properties 122
Richmond and Gordon, *Duke of* 44,
  45-6, 47
Robinson, R. L.
Rose, Alex 96
Rosebery, *Earl of* 66, 73
Ross & Cromarty (County) 26-29
Ross (Family) of Balnagowan 26
Ross, William *Secretary of State for
  Scotland* 34, 34, 78, 97, 113, 124
Rotherwick, *Lord* 72
Roxburgh (County) 83-4
Roxburghe, *Duke of* 51, 69, 76, 83
Royal Botanic Garden, Edinburgh 10
Royal Commission on land: desir-
  ability of 118
Royal Scottish Forestry Society 117
Ruskich 126
Sawmills 99
Scone (Estate) 105
Scotia Agricultural Club 125
'Scotsman' 110. 126
Scott, Frank 11, 62
Scottish Countryside Commission 24

'Scottish Farming' *May 1975* 104
'Scottish Forestry' 96, 126
'Scottish Landowner' 126
Scottish Landowners Federation 113, 116
Scottish National Farmers Union 116
Scottish Standing Committee, first 121
Scourie (Estate) 24
Seafield, *Earl of* 10, 30, 43, 45
Selkirk (County) 74-75
7:84 Theatre Company 24, 50
Shaw Stewart (Family) 70, 70
Shaw Stewart, *Sir* M. R. 70
Shetland 15, 63, 120-1
Shooting
    See Sport, blood
Sinclair (Family) 22
Skibo Castle (Estate) 23
Smith, Prophet 113
Social conditions: late nineteenth century 9
Socialist Government
    See Labour Government
Soils, pan-bound 96
Sorn, *Lord* 72
South Esk (Estate) 105
Southesk, *Earl of* 51
South Uist 47
Speymouth Forest 11
Sport, blood 24, 27, 45, 53, 90-1, 105, 110-2, 114, 122, 125
Sportsmen
    See Sport, blood
Springkell (Estate) 81
Stair (Estate) 81
Stair (Estate) 67, 79
Stair (Family) 79
State Industries
    See nationalised industries for land nationalisation *See* land; nationalisation
Steel, *Sir* Willliam Strang— 75
Steven, Alasdair 13
Steven, H. M. 92
Stewart, Michael 124
Stewart, *Sir* M. R. Shaw— 70
Stirling (County) 65-6
Stirling, *Sir* John 90
Stirling University 60
Stoer (Estate) 24
Strachur, Lochfyne 99
Strang-Steel, *Sir* William 75
Strathmore, *Earl of* 51
Stuart Fotheringham (Family) 53

Subsidies: forestry *See* Forestry: Subsidies
Suisdale (Estate) 122
Superiority, feudal 75, 117, 124-5
Sutherland (County) 23-6
Sutherland, *Countess of* 23
Sutherland, *Duke of* 23, 27, 47, 74, 76
Swann, *Sir* Michael 108
'Swann Report' 108
T.G.W.U. 11
Taylor, Maurice 62
Taylor of Gryfe, *Lord* 95
Taylor, Tom 95
Teindland Forest 11, 43, 45
Thirlestane Castle, Lauder (Estate) 75
Thirlestane (Estate) 74, 75
Thomson, Bell 10
Tillhill Forestry Group 84
Tillicoultry (Estate) 60
Timber ponds 70
Timber production: projected 99
Timber shortage: World War I & II 92, 94
'The Times' 114
Tobacco manufacturers: land interests 27. *See also* Wills (Family)
Torbanehill, Bathgate (Estate) 66
Tory Government
    See Conservative Government
Transport and General Workers union 11
Traquair (Estate) 72, 74
Tulchan (Estate) 51
Tweeddale (Estate) 69, 76
Tweeddale, *Marquis of* 69
Tynninghame (Estate) 69
Uig Crofters Ltd. 31
Uist, South 47
Uniforms: forestry commision 98
Unions: Farm Workers 115
United Free Church Mission 10
University Education: forestry 97-99
University of — See under name of university
Usher (Family) 84
Valuation Roll: Perthshire 111
Vermin
    See also Game 95, 108, 111
Vestey, E. H. 24
Victoria, Queen 47
Wages: forestry commission 99
Wake, Hereward, *Major* 31
Waldegrave, *Lord* 95
Walden, *Lord* Howard de 78

Wardlaw Ramsay, Robert Balfour 60
Welsh, Mr 122
Wemyss & March, *Earl of* 62, 67, 69,
    71, 73, 74
West of Scotland Agricultural College
    107
West Lothian (County) 66-7
Westminster, Duke of 23
Whitbread, W. H. *Col.* 27
Whitley Council 11
Whittinghame (Estate) 27, 69
'Who's Who' 68, 69
Wiggins, Teape & Co. Ltd. 99
Wigtown (County) 79-80
Wills (Family) 27, 42, 44, 46, 54, 93
Wilson, *Mr* 111
Wilson, Messrs, *Timber Merchants,*
    Troon 99
Woodlands, private. *See* Forestry:
    private Estates
Workers Trade Union 11
World War I 92, 94
World War II 92
Wyfold, *Lady* 34
Zetland, *Earl of* 60, 63